T0158016

EDUCATING
A BILLION

Celebrating 35 Years of
Penguin Random House India

EDUCATING A BILLION

HOW EDTECH START-UPS, APPS, YOUTUBE AND AI DISRUPTED EDUCATION

ARJUN MOHAN

PENGUIN
BUSINESS

An imprint of Penguin Random House

PENGUIN BUSINESS

USA | Canada | UK | Ireland | Australia
New Zealand | India | South Africa | China | Singapore

Penguin Business is part of the Penguin Random House group of companies
whose addresses can be found at global.penguinrandomhouse.com

Published by Penguin Random House India Pvt. Ltd
4th Floor, Capital Tower 1, MG Road,
Gurugram 122 002, Haryana, India

First published in Penguin Business by Penguin Random House India 2023

ISBN 9780670099856

Typeset in Adobe Garamond Pro by MAP Systems, Bengaluru, India
Printed at Thomson Press India Ltd, New Delhi

For Meher and Aryan

Contents

Introduction

Right to Education

The modified rickshaw carrying ten people steadily trudged over the freshly asphalted roads, taking us from Raebareli Civil Lines towards villages en route to Amethi. Ashique and I were on our community stint at the Tata Administrative Service (TAS) and were placed with a nongovernmental organization (NGO) supported by one of the Tata Trusts. To my excitement, the NGO was focused on education and was trying to bring kids who had dropped out of school back to formal education. TAS officers are expected to spend three months at an NGO during their probation, learning about the philanthropic side of the group and supporting the NGO with good management practices. During this period, which is termed as 'community stint', some people simply while away their time at the NGO headquarters. So, Rajeshji, the founder of the NGO, was pleasantly surprised when I told him that we wanted to work with the children at the camps rather than sitting in their office. He responded, laughing, 'Someone from the previous batch asked me to inform the Trust office that he was working from Raebareli, his home town, as there was nothing to do here. I will be delighted if you visit the camps, but let me warn you, it's not easy to interact with these children, so don't be disappointed.' I thought: 'He must be talking about Ashique's *mallu* (Malayalam-accented) Hindi; my Hindi is impeccable, thanks to my love for Bollywood and the North Indian girl I was dating (now my wife). Anyway, not a fight worth picking, let's go to the camp.' The NGO ran twenty-odd camps across the districts of Raebareli and Amethi. Rajeshji asked us to go to the nearest one, which was about 10 km away from their headquarters in Raebareli town.

Thus started our journey to one of the camps in a nearby village. Since there was literally no public transport to make use of the good roads of the town—constructed thanks to the VIP MP of the constituency—the resourceful entrepreneurs of the area had modified their goods autos into informal public transit vehicles that can squeeze in ten passengers. The highlight of our trip was the free commentary provided as we passed by a huge house built on a mustard farm. 'That's the guest house where Soniaji [Sonia Gandhi] and family stay when they visit the constituency. Built especially for them a few years ago. Priyankaji [Priyanka Gandhi Vadra] visits almost every month these days. Look carefully, you may be lucky enough to get a peek.' The regular visits may have been due to the premonition she had about the difficult elections the ruling party was going to face in 2014. The tall walls ensure you see nothing.

We paid the driver Rs 5 after getting down and started our walk on the kutcha road to the camp, which was 2 km away from the main road. Thanks to Rajeshji's introduction, we were welcomed by the site manager, Vijay, a man in his late forties. The camp was being run in a small building which had one large hall where classes were going on. There were twelve kids in the age group of eight to ten years, who had dropped out of standards I to V. They were trying to run a curriculum which would give the kids the confidence to get the basics of math, language and science right, and hence go back to a class which would be right for their current age. Ashique and I were amazed at the warm manner in which everyone interacted with us and their innocence. We had absolutely no problem interacting with the kids who could talk only in Hindi, and if one could speak with a bit of colloquial style, it worked well. As with most kids, teaching them math was a struggle and kids lost interest very quickly though it was basic math, such as addition and multiplication. The camp keepers who doubled as teachers were trying their best to hold their interest and attention but with little success.

After over an hour of intense study, it was time for lunch. Food was cooked at the camp and students lived in the same building through the two-month camp. The break was for an hour, but in ten minutes, the children finished their lunch and ran outside. Vijay grimaced, 'Now they will be off doing what they like the most. Give them five hours every day and still they will ask for more.' Curious, I walked out to see what they were up to. They were all huddled around a kid sitting on a haystack with a small mobile phone which had a tiny screen. They were playing videos from Bollywood movies on a feature mobile phone using a 2G connection. The framed video and music were able to sustain their interest without any struggle. An idea struck me.

With Vijay's permission, in the second half, I asked the children if they wanted to learn math like the Bollywood songs they devoured. To puzzled looks, I opened my laptop and played a video on addition we had done at BYJU'S as part of our new project on online learning. The video was in English, and I was worried the kids wouldn't find it interesting since their fluency in English was subpar. To my surprise, there was pin-drop silence for half an hour as the presenter in the video went about explaining how numbers are added with the help of sleek animation which flashed on the screen. The kids loved the video and asked for more, to which I promised I would keep coming back and introducing them to such new things. When I asked Vijay why they didn't make use of such tech tools to educate the kids, he responded saying, 'We get electricity only for two hours every day.' I made a mental note to speak to Rajeshji about introducing tech tools to educate these kids and ways to do the same. As both the children and staff appeared happy with the video session, what could be the deterrent then? Access? Affordability?

I whipped out my mobile and typed a WhatsApp text to Byju: 'I just did a field testing of the online product, and I am sold that we are on to something really big.' Then I realized my Airtel connection didn't have network in the village. I decided I should talk to him once I was back in Raebareli.

Chapter 1

Educating a Billion

We are a nation of 1.4 billion people as of 2022. Of this figure, 260 million are school-going children, the largest anywhere in the world, and around 36 million are studying in colleges and universities at any given point in time.[1]

According to the National Statistical Office survey 2017–18, India's adult literacy rate, i.e., literacy among a billion people above fifteen years of age, is 81 per cent.[2] This number is below the global average of 86.3 per cent by more than 5 per cent. Dig deeper and you will see that our urban literacy rate is close to China's national literacy rate of 96.4 per cent and our rural literacy rate as close to Pakistan's 58 per cent.[3] We can always justify this by stating that we are a young republic and making continuous progress.

The National Literacy Mission defines literacy as the ability to read, write and do arithmetic and apply the same

---

[1] AISHE 2020-21, Department of Higher Education, https://aishe.gov.in/aishe/gotoAisheReports.

[2] Household Social Consumption on Education 2017-18, National Statistical Office MSPI, GoI, https://ourworldindata.org/literacy (page 1).

[3] UNESCO Institute of Statistics | CIA World factbook, https://worldpopulationreview.com/

1

to one's daily life. Let me share an anecdote on literacy. On 18 April 1991, Chelakkodan Aysha, a sixty-year-old Muslim woman who was illiterate till her sixties, declared Kerala as a 100 per cent literate state when she became the last person in the state to turn literate—symbolically reading her name. Kerala's tryst with literacy is eons old and has been built systematically over centuries through successive dispensations—local Hindu rulers in Travancore, Christian missionaries and even Muslim rulers in the north. Literacy in India has been implemented as the skill to just read and write one's name in their mother tongue; Aysha did a lot more by passing Class XII at the age of sixty by dint of hard work for almost two years.

Over the years, she lost her ability to read and write to old age and so did Kerala its 100 per cent literacy metric. Currently, the state's literacy rate is 91 per cent. The obvious question we all should be asking is: does the act of basic reading and writing create an educated class that can contribute to nation-building? Being educated means a lot more than becoming literate, and educated citizens are what our nation needs to take our quality of living to the next level, to help move more of our population out of poverty. To be educated in this complex world, it is necessary to get access to high-quality and technical higher education. Only an educated population will help our nation reap the demographic dividend, i.e., the phase in a nation's life when the number of people who can work is higher than those who cannot. India entered the demographic dividend opportunity in 2005–06 and is expected to remain in that position till 2055–56. However, our statistics are not impressive when it comes to educating our population.

Our teacher–student ratio is 1:42 and the quality of these teachers, each expected to teach forty-two students on an average, is a concern. Northern and central parts of our country are particularly facing this deficiency. Not only teachers, the infrastructure at our schools and colleges is poor too. In fact, a majority of the rural schools don't not even have access to clean sanitation facilities. Expecting India to educate a billion minds for the future with this ecosystem is akin to expecting a miracle.

A similar situation exists in our universities and colleges. With several liberalization policies being implemented in university education, the Government of India tried to expand the footprint of higher education only to see it fall short of expectations. Our gross enrolment ratio (GER) is one of the lowest in the world at 29 per cent (as of 2022) and not even half of what a developing nation like ours should have. Though the policies and investments have tried to solve for access and affordability, the issue of quality is something the government has never been able to solve due to the lack of passionate teachers interested in making the learner truly educated.

In this book, I will argue that the solution to educating a billion lies *online* with the help of technology and not really by building more bricks-and-mortar schools and universities. We are not an economy with so much of surplus to invest in building thousands of university campuses while the real problem is of quality of delivery. I will take you through the origins and paths followed by companies in Indian edtech and how they are progressively trying to solve this problem with technology. Broadly, the journey will can be divided into four phases:

- The 1990s and 2000s: First attempt at using technology at scale in schools and companies like Educomp, Digimate by HP and Next Education created products to make teachers more effective. At the same time, consumer play or selling directly to consumers in India was attempted by Meritnation and internationally by TutorVista.

- 2010–20: Growth of edtech as an alternative to conventional education with deployment of technology and media tools in a big way in education. The story will invariably end up tracking the hero of this phase—BYJU'S. How BYJU'S innovated, scaled and cracked the market is the story of edtech in India itself. Its success spawned more companies like Unacademy and Vedantu, and more innovation in the segment. Their stories will explain newer pathways which opened up in edtech.

- 2020–21: How the industry became the mainstay of education when Covid-19 shut down all conventional mediums of education—schools, colleges, coaching centres. The explosion in growth which came with Covid-19 blinded the organizations which tried to grow at all cost rather than focus on delivering quality education. Traditional educators were forced to adopt technology, creating a hybrid version which started gaining popularity. A new segment within edtech—university education and working professional education—started growing, thanks to the tailwind of Covid-19. We will tell this story through the eyes of upGrad, an underdog in the segment which built itself as a winner during the Covid-19 years.

- 2021 onwards: Edtech in the post-Covid-19 world and how things looked like when the dust settled. Painful cuts were made and business models rewritten. Admist all this, interestingly, online learning started becoming a mainstream option along with conventional learning.

Edtech was not the only segment in India to get digitalized in the recent past. It was one of many; retail, transportation and financial services went through this journey a little earlier. In a way, the last decade can be considered a decade of digitalization for India. Alongside technology and globalization, capital provided by private entities played an important role in this revolution.

Hence, the story of India's edtech is also invariably the story of venture capital in Indian start-up sectors. It is ironic that a tightly controlled segment of our economy in which the government pumps around 5 per cent of its budget every year needed risk capital from venture capitalists (VCs) abroad to achieve big growth and propagate quality education. These funds didn't make their way to India for no reason. In our nation—the most populous in the world—development has touched just a small fraction of the population. Due to this reason, it promises to provide high returns to investment for risk capital in technology-backed companies. The 'promise' is also fraught with risks. So, investments typically happen when money is available cheap to invest. It is interesting to track the correlation of US fed rates—one of the sharpest indicators of cheap money globally—with the period of prosperous money flow into Indian start-ups.

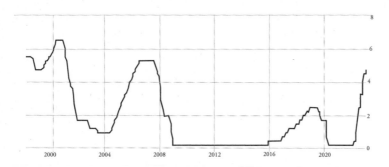

Fed rates 1995–2023
Tradingeconomics.com | Federal Reserve

Observe the period 2009 to 2016 and then the Covid-19 years. The fed rates, or the rates at which commercial banks in the US can borrow funds, was close to zero. More about this later.

For now, just understand it as lot of cheap money available in the developed world and thanks to slow population growth in these countries, not much investment options.

Above everything else, this book is the story of India's new generation of entrepreneurs—the ones who are full of hope, who never doubt their abilities and simply don't know what fear is. The book is about their vision, audacity and optimism that's changing the education system after 200-plus years of slumber.

Chapter 2

Passion, Devotion and Inspiration

Sunday Morning Trailer

The auditorium of Jyoti Nivas College was full of Common Admission Test (CAT) aspirants on that chilly morning in January 2008. Nearly 500 seats were filled, mostly with working professionals who were there to know more about the contemporary upstart of the Master of Business Administration (MBA) coaching industry. Most made the trip leaving their warm beds on that Sunday morning out of amusement generated by an audacious ad on the front page of a daily—an ad which claimed to teach shortcuts to crack CAT questions in seconds.

My tryst with CAT and the Indian Institutes of Management (IIMs) began in my engineering college, National Institute of Technology Calicut (NITC). The bug of management bit me there and I made up my mind to do an MBA. Since the IIMs are the best place to do an MBA in India, I started my preparation for CAT while I was in my final year of college. Back then, CAT was considered one of the most competitive examinations in the world. Around 2,00,000 aspirants appeared for CAT to get admission into a paltry 2000 seats offered by six IIMs, making the selection possible only if you were in the top 1 per cent. Hence, it was all about scoring a

98+ percentile and then cracking the equally competitive group discussion and personal interview (GDPI) rounds. As a small-town boy who gained confidence in talking in any language other than Malayalam only while I was in college, I found the exam uncrackable when I appeared for it the first time in 2006. Not someone to give up that easily, I continued my preparation after joining my job at Bengaluru. I was not alone in my journey of perseverance; there were ten others from my class at NITC who flunked the CAT, came to Bengaluru and decided to prepare again.

The name Byju appeared in our Mallu (NITC Malayali alumni) email group for the first time in 2007 when RGC (abbreviation for Rakesh George Cherian) sent out a glowing email recommending Byju and his CAT classes to all of us. The first reaction of a Malayali who sees a local Kerala name like Byju alongside CAT, where rankers are decided based on their English proficiency, is to laugh. So RGC became the laughing stock for his recommendation and the episode was quickly forgotten. Few weeks later, after a particularly hard TIME mock CAT, RGC and I were discussing the Data Interpretation (DI) caselets. For a particularly hard question on Venn diagrams, RGC showed an approach of replacing circles with lines and solving the question a lot more easily. I didn't really understand the approach and chose to ignore it since anyway after all that, RGC ended up selecting the wrong option. Nevertheless, he gave credit to Byju. 'But you got the answer wrong, dude,' I told him. He responded, 'Doesn't matter. The approach works, I might have made some silly mistake. This is not for me.' Neither Byju nor CAT left me, and I again found him on page 1 of a daily in 2008. The ugly amateurish yellow ad on the front page was unmissable! The fact that it was amateurish would have increased its read rate. The ad had five complex

CAT math questions and a call-out to come and attend a free session on Sunday morning if you wanted to learn how to solve such complex problems through shortcuts. 'Perfect thing to do on a Sunday morning for singles,' I thought. The ad had a phone number to register yourself with basic details—name, email ID, college from where you graduated. I told myself, 'Let me try this out' and sent the details. Next afternoon, I got a call from the number I had sent the details to. The caller started speaking in Malayalam. 'You are Arjun, right, from NIT Calicut? I'm Byju. Lot of your classmates have studied in my class: Sajid, RGC, Anilesh, Raghav, etc. Most of them cracked CAT last year. Looking forward to meeting you on Sunday.' He went right down to business. I thought, 'A teacher who calls every customer who registered for a free session and ensures they turn up. That's wow! Is he a teacher or a businessman? Why can't one be both anyway.'

Bang at 9 a.m. a tall, dark and handsome young man walked in and introduced himself in his thick Mallu accent: 'Good morning, I'm Byju. I have written CAT twice and got 100 percentile in both my attempts. First attempt, I went for the A, B and C interviews and cracked them all. I realized that there is a bigger business in this and hence decided not to go to IIMs to study business. Next few hours, I am going to give you all a trailer on how you can learn to crack CAT or any competitive examination.' Two things anyone will observe about Byju in the first 10 minutes itself is his inexhaustible energy and deep passion for whatever he is doing. It's almost as if teaching is his devotion.

The next four hours he ploughed through previous years' CAT papers and showcased usage of his shortcut techniques across years and sections. Every time he solved complex questions in a fraction of a minute, he highlighted his methodology through the stylish movement of his stylus on the tablet screen which was getting projected and the statistic to go with it. He peppered his session with well-timed one-liners, captivating students throughout. The session, which he called a trailer or demo, was nothing short of a performance—an orchestra of math or was it a math musical; he actually tried to rap in the middle with lyrics made up on arithmetic and geometric progression formulas. Not everyone was as taken by the idea as me—to few, it was all Greek and Latin and they looked bored and a couple of them were fighting their sleep. In the most embarrassing moment close to the end, a student sitting in the second row who was asleep found the math musical so lullaby-ic that he fell into a slumber so deep that he literally fell off his chair into the aisle. The roar of laughter woke everyone up. Any teacher would have gotten embarrassed with something like that. Not the performer Byju. He smiled and said, 'My classes and CAT are not for everyone. You need to have a love for numbers. I have seen that engineers pick it up well. Others will need some effort.'

Weekends with Math

The session by Byju was the best session in math I have ever attended. In the garb of shortcuts, he was making fun of the way we have learned math all our life at school. Rather than going by the curricular methods of formulas, derivation and equations to solve the questions, Byju was asking you to simply use the multiple-choice answer options to hack your way to the answer. He commented, 'They have given you options; use it and get to the answers quickly.' The interesting part was how he codified the entire approach and created a course using it that covers the complete CAT syllabus, which basically was Class X math syllabus. He was fundamentally mocking the education system in the signature Byju's way—gently. I walked up to the maestro and introduced myself. 'You are Arjun Mohan from NITC. How was the session?' he asked curiously. I told him it was brilliant, and that I have decided to join the batch. He smiled and moved on to speak to the next person waiting to talk to him. On my way out, I met Riju, Byju's brother and his one-man support/finance/operations organization. 'Where are you from in Kerala?' he enquired. When I told him I hail from Kannur and the exact village name where my house is located, we realized that our hometowns are just 5 km apart. Soon, I realized that though Byju operated alone, he was supported by a small group of Riju's friends, who helped conduct the operations every weekend at Jyoti Nivas College. The motley crew of young men were mostly from the Azhikode–Pallikkunnu villages in Kannur and I quickly became one of them, helping Byju and Riju with the classes every weekend in Bengaluru. Another person who was part of the team from the early days was Divya, BYJU's co-founder and later Byju's wife. She was an integral part of the brand's growth story and handled multiple roles, from teaching and delivery to later brand strategy and public relations (PR).

I used to love Byju's sessions. He conducted all the quant and data sessions, which I devoured, while the verbal sessions by his partner Santosh weren't that exciting for me. So, I asked him if I could attend sessions with all his batches which used to happen in Bengaluru. He said, 'You can. Then you will master the techniques real quick. Why don't you put it to some use? Our batch sizes are increasing and the number of people coming with doubts between the sessions are also going up. I want you to start solving doubts between the classes.'

I was overjoyed at the prospect of working with Byju, who by then had become an inspiration for me.

We worked hard all our weekends—in fact, Sajesh, who's Riju's friend, and I, juggled our day jobs with it. The classes usually started at 8 a.m. and went on till 8 p.m. The organization grew at a spectacular pace and so did Byju's fame and fortune. We were happy working for our 'Sir' and enjoyed our weekends with friends while creating value for aspirants.

Finally, the D-day arrived, and I did well in the math portion of the CAT exam, but my verbal didn't go well. 'It's hard to get calls when you have only attempted eleven questions in verbal,' Byju told me post the paper. I was disheartened. Byju continued, 'Anyway, there are much better things to do here than going for an IIM. Join me full time. I think there is so much more to do.' He was wrong, I got all eleven of my verbal questions right and hence managed to clear the cut-off for verbal. And with my stellar percentile in Quant and DI, I got a few IIM calls too.

The best part about getting some calls is the free invites to GDPI boot camps from top coaching institutes. The practice was created by coaching institutes to claim the success of 100 percentilers and achievers who make it to the top IIMs. Since these people ended up taking coaching in the form of GDPI preparation with these coaching institutes, they become their students and the institutes can claim credit for their success. These names, along with their pictures, make their way to newspapers and pamphlets. This is how some of the top rank holders appear in all the top institutes' promotional ads. Boot camps by TIME and Career Launcher inspired me to do something similar at BYJU'S and I suggested the same to him. Byju the visionary jumped at the idea and thus started our knowledge download sessions. The turnout we had was limited and since we had put in a lot of effort designing the sessions, we came up with the idea of recording the same and posting it on our YouTube channel. That was the first instance of video making at BYJU'S. Though nobody really tracked the views or engagement of those videos, Byju made a note of the way videos were able to seamlessly replicate the same impact of a star teacher.[4]

Teaching Gig

Byju was clear that he wanted to scale up and expand across the country—multiple courses, cities, etc. So, like me, he got few more of his ex-students lined up to join him. IIM Bangalore was not impressed when I failed to answer questions on electrical engineering control systems in the selection interview and hence, I decided not to go for my MBA that year. 'Sir, if you just want me to teach and solve doubts, it doesn't make any sense joining full time. I can easily do it along with my job and my salary will be an unnecessary burden on the company,' I told him then. 'I want you to take evening classes on weekdays in some colleges around Bangalore. Will you be able to do it along with your day job?' Thus started my teaching gig which I ran alongside my day job as an electronic design automation (EDA) consultant at Mentor Graphics. Having a teaching job alongside your regular job is a common thing in Kerala and hence this arrangement didn't seem odd to either me or Byju. This is one way education enterprises in the state get access to

---

4 Education and Careers Desk, 'Everyone Taught Tanisha: Why Same Topper's Face Appears on Multiple Coaching Centre Ads', News18, 6 October 2022, https://www.news18.com/news/education-career/everyone-taught-tanisha-why-same-toppers-face-appears-on-multiple-coaching-centre-ads-6098545.html

quality teachers at low cost and in my view is a model which should be widely used to help start-ups attain quality and high standards at fraction of a cost.

The classes were mostly on weekends in and around Bengaluru and I thoroughly enjoyed mimicking Byju's style and methods and wowing the students preparing for CAT. It was just not the classes; it was how the entire structure worked. Every session was improvised so much that it turned into a mini demo session and at every session, we asked impressed students to get their friends to attend a free session and see if they want to join. They happily obliged. To ensure people didn't feel they had missed out anything, the first eight sessions were kept independent of each other, i.e., now a student could start his BYJU'S coaching in any one of the first eight sessions and we had eight weeks after starting of the batch to fill the batch. By the ninth session, we ensured that with extra classes and compressed schedules, the student was up to speed. The remaining eight sessions were a combination of applications from the first eight. Our batches were a roaring success, and we could really see that we were on to something big. Well, not big enough.

'CAT is a small market and the number of students taking it is stuck at 2 lakh. Of this, hardly 1 lakh is serious and not more than 50,000 will ever pay for coaching. Of that 50,000, 30,000 won't do more than the mock CAT, so our actual addressable market is 20,000 students. At Rs 30,000 fees, the total money we can ever make is Rs 60 crore. We can't build a multi-crore education company with this; we will have to crack bigger exams,' Byju lamented in one of our strategy meetings which usually happened over dinner at Coast2Coast—a Mangalore-cuisine restaurant famous for its spicy fish and ghee roast chicken. 'Our USP is our shortcuts and there is only limited application of the same in exams like JEE and Medical entrance. JEE Mains and state-level engineering exams, possibly yes, but it will need some work. Physics and math, we can handle between us; what do we do for chemistry,' I asked. 'Start working on a curriculum and see how to do it in physics and math; for chemistry we will recruit someone who can teach it like us,' Byju's thoughts were already racing ahead while responding.

Diversifying the Techniques

Trying to apply BYJU'S shortcuts to the physics and math syllabus of JEE Mains and various state engineering entrances was not very straightforward. This was because the papers were different; unlike CAT, these questions were not tricky and hence the prospect of hacking was limited. Most papers had hardly 5–10 per cent questions where our shortcut techniques could be directly applied. So, we started developing new techniques customized for Class XI and XII physics and math. The first version of the curriculum was ready soon and Byju was happy to run the pilot. The pilot was not exactly a pilot, he wanted to do five batches across five different cities in Kerala and have 1000 students learning from us. I was speechless. We were two teachers and didn't even have a chemistry teacher. 'How are we going to do this?' 'We should first figure out how to do a splash across Kerala with a marketing campaign,' he continued, 'which will give us 1000 students. Do you know anyone in Manorama? We should team up with them.' Though my question was never answered, I heard myself answering 'let me try'.

Media houses love events. They get paid for writing a few articles and unsellable ad spaces in the name of association. A high-level contact I found in Manorama agreed to associate

with a virtually unknown coaching company on the back of
the pitch given by its inspiring founder and the idea. There
still existed one problem—the company did not really
have a marketable name. Think & Learn Pvt. Ltd was a
name conjured out of thin air by one of the people in that
discussion. Everyone loved it and hence our first Manorama
Think & Learn scholarship test was launched. The test was
planned on back-to-back three days in five cities. We drove
from the northern town of Kannur to the southern city capital
of Thiruvananthapuram conducting demos for students who
came to learn how to hack the questions which came in the
scholarship test, strategically placing the demo session by Byju
immediately after the scholarship test. Of the five cities we
conducted demos in, we were able to start batches in two cities.
Kochi especially was a big batch with seventy-five students. But
the problem of the chemistry teacher remained. As the date
of the batch approached, I became increasingly spooked and
started posting ads on teacher forums. I hated chemistry in
my high school days, and I found it painful interviewing and
sitting through demos of these chemistry teachers. I had to do
it all and finally gave an offer to someone who seemed to know
some inorganic chemistry.

Conducting classes in Kerala gave me first-hand experience
on how to run a one-man enterprise—literally. I used to
prepare the practice sheets, print them and carry them with
me to Kerala in a bus for which I had booked tickets. I booked
the hotel, booked the college classroom for classes and carried
the Daily Practice Problems (DPPs) and class-sheets to class.
I'm not exactly sure what impression I created in front of my
students when I carried the podium and projector screen to
set up the class first and then started teaching. However, they
never complained. The delivery and content as usual received

full marks, and we achieved the unthinkable for the first batch of a new institute—a student cracked JEE and joined an IIT. However, our operations in Kerala were below par and thanks to all the ad hoc ways in which we operated, we started getting negative feedback and we eventually had to shut down the Kerala batch. Byju never blamed me and asked me to focus on the Bengaluru batch, which was a roaring success. Somewhere within, he knew that I had tried to salvage things and there was no real support. The experience in Kerala would become the hallmark of BYJU'S—blitz marketing, push sales, audacious promises, differentiated content, unique teaching techniques, exceptional teachers and below average operations.

Chapter 3

The Midnight Idea

It is said that every great change starts with one individual. Someone who is 'overconfident' enough to challenge the age-old norms and show it to the world that they are better. Towards 2010, India was finally getting such confident youngsters. The Indian economy was doing well under our economist prime minister and scientist President. And the world was looking at India and China as stories of the future.

Dhoni and his men had just brought home the ICC T20 World Cup trophy beating Pakistan in the final; home-grown PSLV had just created a record by launching ten satellites in one launch; the automotive world was looking closely at a revolutionary car worth $2500 called Nano, which the Tatas had just launched; and Sachin and Binny had just left their jobs as developers at Amazon to start their online bookstore, which they called Flipkart. Successful Indians were returning home from the US to establish dotcom 2.0 companies or outsourcing units of US companies. India was the nuclear superpower where every multinational wanted to start their development office, and we were a generation of confident youngsters who believed we were destined to rewrite the world order. Even the impact of the 2008 financial crisis was limited, and business was looking good.

Crash Course

Our focus moved to servicing JEE Mains and Karnataka engineering entrance students in Bengaluru, which in itself was a large business. I learned from our mistakes in Kerala and began focusing more on academics, now ably supported by an ops team under Riju. The classes were well received, and we started to apply the growth hacks from CAT batches to grow. The first one was to create multiple batches of various durations and speed of delivery to cater to student cohorts that learn at various paces. A crash course for students who wanted to do last-minute preparation before the exam was one of our most popular offerings. For the crash-course batch, we planned on a grand scale and booked one of the largest auditoriums in Bengaluru which could accommodate 2000 students at a time. The well-oiled BYJU'S marketing machinery was able to sign up students at scale and we had a full house even before the batch started. I was finally excited about making a profit with such a large scale.

The first class had very good feedback and I was surprised to see Byju disturbed that evening. He shared his thoughts: 'After acquisition cost, teacher's pay, transportation, hall, admin, etc., we will hardly make any money. In fact, I think we will lose money. There is no business model here. Worst part is that our marketing was so successful and generated so many enquiries but we are not able to cater to all of them due to restricted seats.' 'Is there anything we can do about it now; can we look at starting one more batch?' I asked. 'That won't work,' he continued, 'it will add more cost and we won't be able to deliver the best quality as we have only Anita, Anuj, you and I who can take classes the way we want.' 'Did you observe the class today, there were hardly any doubts raised by the students. If we have mastered the content so well, why should we keep repeating the same things? Can you record what you are teaching and why don't we sell the content to the students who didn't get seats?' The more I thought about it, the more it made sense. 'But, Sir, this means we have to record all sessions of the crash course in the next twenty days because the market will be over for this year with exam date round the corner, plus very few kids of this age will have a computer to see these videos and there will be the complication of piracy.' Byju was ready with the solution. 'We will sell the entire content with a tab and since it goes with a tab, we will be able to command a price premium too and yes, in the next twenty days, you will have to record every night till midnight,' he smiled. 'I will; just ensure others also do the same.' There was no smile left when I replied.

The idea of recording every evening post my day job and morning classes was taxing, and the midnight timeline mostly extended well past 2 a.m. But the excitement of creating India's first video learning product kept us going.

Regular curriculum has a lot of faff so when one is preparing for a competitive exam, the best approach is to focus on key concepts and cut the faff. So, when you teach mechanics, you teach the kids free body diagram first—a concept which doesn't even figure in Class XI and XII syllabus of most boards but can make solving the statics questions easy. This is the essence of a good crash course. We tried to replicate our exact crash course in these recordings. Each chapter started with a rapid revision of the most frequently asked questions, practicals and application-level concepts and then drilled down on extensions and application of the same through hundreds of previous years' questions which we solved mostly with our trademark shortcuts. We made it dramatic with frequent references to the amount of time, space and energy taken to solve a question using conventional methods and leveraged the touchscreen to gesture the superiority of our methods. A lot of focus was on making the product comprehensive so that a student who starts his or her preparation late can simply use our product to cover the entire curriculum relevant to the exam in the shortest possible time. In other words, we created a modern-day boot camp version of a two-year-long coaching course. After twenty days of intense work, the product was ready, thanks to the parallel editing effort of Vinay and team, who had by then taken over the entire content and editing departments of the company. We tried to be conservative with our projections and burnt just sixty tabs. Byju insisted on keeping the pricing of the tab same as the crash-course-in-class fee—Rs 25,000. He shrewdly calculated that so close to examination, most desperate students will pick the product and the price elasticity will be low.

Next day, we invited the students who didn't get seats to the batch and gave them the demo of the tab. The pitch was: exact same sessions by same teachers but with the flexibility to learn when they want to. Flexibility was super important for students since we were very close to the exam date. We sold the sixty tabs that afternoon with a few more in pre-order since there were students who wanted to buy, but we didn't have the units. We promised to get them the tabs next day after burning these overnight. Thus, the first online product from BYJU'S staple helped some extremely self-motivated and last-minute students hit their exam halls with confidence. Along with the small profit we made, we were delighted to see the testimonials we got post the exam on how the razor-sharp sessions focusing on key concepts and hacks that can be readily used in the exam helped them prepare well in a limited amount of time.

'This proves my hypothesis right,' Byju proclaimed. 'A good teacher can comprehensively and effectively teach students through videos. It not only solves our problem of limited rockstar teachers, but it also solves a big issue for students in smaller towns and villages who don't have access to the best teachers. Teachers are finally the reason why classes are engaging and students learn. Imagine the impact you can create in the life and career of a student in a town like Kannur if he's given access to a top JEE teacher while in Class XI and XII.' 'He is right,' I thought. 'I had only heard about IITs and JEE when I went for the Kerala entrance coaching at PC Thomas during my Class XI term break. The biggest reason why small-town kids don't make it to these prestigious institutions is not lack of talent but lack of exposure and training. Video learning could really flatten the world of education.' 'We will go big on this,' he continued. 'I'm planning to expand our K-12 [education for children from kindergarten through twelfth grade] business in a big way—both online and offline—and we will soon be a multi-crore company.'

Growth needs investment, and till that point, Byju had thought about using the excess cash generated from his successful CAT enterprise to grow the business. The idea of fundraising for start-ups was not mainstream in India then, and hence not in consideration. However, all this was going to change soon.

Coffee at the Campus Town

Byju got introduced to the idea through a chance meeting with Aarin Capital run by Manipal founder Ranjan Pai and Infosys ex-CFO Mohandas Pai. We used to run a batch for Manipal students to help them crack CAT. The sessions used to happen at the Fortune hotel ballroom on the Manipal campus. The venue was an expensive choice for the stage we were at, but that's how Byju did things. We ensured that he pushed hard and hustled and the overflowing multiple batches paid multifold of the venue rental. The biggest return however was not the student turnout but a chance encounter with the founder Ranjan Pai. The story goes that Ranjan, who was visiting Manipal and staying at Fortune hotel, saw a big rush of students at 6 p.m. moving towards the ballroom. He was surprised to know that students were running to attend the classes of a guy who was training them for CAT, that too in the evening class. Super intrigued, the founder of Aarin took a sneak peek of the classes and like anyone else was amazed at the energy of the teacher and engagement of the students for a math class. He didn't waste time and asked the hotel manager to leave a message for Byju to meet him the next day. Next morning, over a coffee at the campus town, he met Byju and discussed investing in his company. There could be nothing more poetic—one of India's oldest and largest educational entrepreneurs (Manipal) meeting the new-age educational entrepreneur in the campus town built around education business. The conversation that day at one of India's largest offline campuses was a lot about how Byju should grow his business to the digital world.[5]

However, when Byju decided to take money from Aarin Capital, the thesis was not online education. The idea was to expand into K-10, K-12 and Union Public Service Commission (UPSC) test prep businesses where the teaching would be done in the way Byju was teaching for CAT. The online idea remained an R&D idea which kept getting tinkered by the new recruits he had hired in the company. Still working part time, I was the outlier amidst the new full-time employees who

5   Anshul Dhamija, 'Ranjan Pai: The benevolent investor', *Forbes*, 13 July 2017, https://www.forbesindia.com/article/startups/ranjan-pai-the-benevolent-investor/47527/1

now were running the show and making operational decisions. Though I was enamoured by Byju the entrepreneur and his vision, the 23-year-old me couldn't take the plunge of joining him full time after leaving a well-paid job at Mentor Graphics, a multinational company that made simulation software. Blame it on my middle-class upbringing! By then, a few of his students who had been working part time with him earlier, like me, had joined full time. As the only old-time part-time employee, I felt increasingly out of place. CAT 2009 came and went, and this time, I decided to take the offer from IIM Kozhikode and enrol for an MBA. That was my first break from BYJU'S or at least I thought so—unbeknownst.

The thesis of online learning at BYJU's, however, was growing green shoots. There were few individuals in the new hires Byju brought into the company who saw the potential in the online thesis and who continued the experimentation— notably Vinay and Aanand. With the support of an enthusiastic Byju, they continued the experimentation with multiple formats of editing, making the videos richer with 2D and 3D elements and an engaging storytelling style. While progress was made online, the offline K-12 business was haemorrhaging. Offline centre management is about two things: centre operations and teacher management. Think & Learn was struggling on both fronts. Feedback plummeted and the new-age organization couldn't really manage the teachers with their own hardened perspective of life. Unable to let things continue the same way, Vinay started relying on old-timers like me again. Soon, it became a weekly routine for me to take the Friday evening bus from Kozhikode to Bengaluru, take classes on Saturday and Sunday and return by the Sunday evening bus. While the schedule ensured I didn't have much of a social life at IIMK, I thoroughly enjoyed teaching and making some extra bucks which could pay for my MBA. Once again, the Bengaluru days got me closer to Byju, Vinay, Aanand and online education, and I started getting into product and content development again.

Early Days of the Learning App

Large-scale consumer usage of a product only starts after the product has gone through multiple iterations. The process typically takes years for an online product. People and media normally only see the viral growth and adoption in the final stages and celebrate the product and company as an overnight success. The truth is that an 'overnight success' takes about a decade in the making. The long and arduous journey involves multiple builds, user testing, consumer feedback and a million iterations to take the product to where it becomes acceptable to the customers.

We developed the product with sharp insights from some of the best and most experienced teachers, based on what they learned from teaching thousands of students across this country. Thanks to the offline classrooms, we could get immediate feedback. The in-between versions were given to students in our classrooms, slowly growing the online content as the USP of our classes. With its large investment in classrooms and online, like any other typical start-up, Think & Learn moved to red from black and had to rely on investor capital. This is the toughest phase in the growth of a start-up—the phase where you are building the product, investing and do not yet have a great brand to attract talent. The churn is typically high in this struggling period and often the founder finds himself alone and wanting to give up. This is one reason why investors prefer companies with multiple founders since they know the struggle if it's just one person. Meanwhile, I completed my MBA and joined TAS. My job with Tatas took me across India in my first year, but I religiously came back to Bengaluru every Friday evening to do my recordings and work on the product.

Byju meanwhile was working with superhuman effort to keep everything running. His CAT business, though not growing, was very profitable and was still funding the new businesses. He was pretty much doing the entire marketing and delivery himself to keep the margins high. He was also managing the offline UPSC and K-12 businesses and trying to grow the same and reduce cost. In parallel, he was trying to find ways to monetize the online content we were generating. The effort to find customers for the online product forced Byju into multiple experimentations. He decided against the franchise model followed by Meritnation, an active player in the online learning space then, since he had burnt his fingers with franchisees once earlier. The ace salesman in Byju got to work and tried to forge partnerships which could help him reach his customers. In outreaches with various retail giants, original equipment manufacturers (OEMs) and school chains, he presented his audacious vision and the pilot product as game changers which could rewrite the way education is done in India.

Of all the pitches he made, one giant OEM was impressed with his vision—Samsung Electronics. Samsung at that time was trying to find use-cases for their tablet business and education seemed like an obvious one. There was just one problem: Samsung wasn't a content company, at least not in India and didn't have the resources to do it at the pace they were looking at. Enter Byju and his dream of making learning accessible across the country through content loaded on a tab. The partnership seemed to be made in heaven. Samsung selected

Byju as one of the top potential partners for their business and flew him to Seoul to present his vision to the global team; Byju did the rest of the work of impressing the Samsung bosses. Back in India, Byju entered into an agreement with Samsung to sell the online product exclusively on Samsung tabs. As part of the deal, Samsung and Byju released educational tabs for various competitive exams and school grades. Samsung, with its almost infinite budget, took care of the marketing and released full front-page advertisements for BYJU'S products in top daily newspapers. The educational tab debuted at Samsung stores, and Byju even deputed some sales guys to stand in stores and give demos to customers to sell the product.

The partnership didn't pan out as planned, and everyone in it quickly realized that the potential of selling education to people walking into Samsung stores was limited. In time, Samsung also pivoted to larger signature stores in limited numbers and started focusing on multi-brand outlets and e-commerce channels more. However, our product didn't fade away like this experiment because quite clearly, it was an idea whose time had arrived.

The years 2010 to 2015, when we worked on the product, were also transformative years for competitive exams in India. One after another, competitive exams started going online—CAT, JEE Mains, JEE Adv, state engineering, medical exams—making the proposition of an online tutoring product like BYJU'S more relevant to a student preparing for the exam. Byju had by then completely changed his focus from CAT to K-12 entrance exams since he saw the CAT exams plateauing and was clearly interested only in spending his time on growing markets. The same business sense helped him see the trend of students moving online much before anyone else. This made him wholeheartedly support the effort within the company to focus on the online product. However, by 2014, a stagnant K-12 classroom business and slow progress of online product development was raising serious questions in my mind about the survival of the business by the time the product would be ready. However, unbeknownst to me, the founder had a plan and this time it was bigger.

Chapter 4

Building Brand BYJU'S:
Fall in Love with Learning

Historically, private enterprises in India grew slowly. Capital was always lacking and investments for growth came either from the owner's personal/family wealth, bank loans or government grants. A company took an entrepreneur's entire lifetime to reach a reasonable scale. Bank loans and grants from government were only available to a connected few. Since the number of entrepreneurs were so few and chances of success so low, these risk-loving wealth creators were often looked down upon by our culture which believed that a job is the best path to prosperity for a capable person. Post-Independence India, controlled by the license raj regime, even forced these people to resort to unethical practices to get access to cheap capital, giving rise to the lexicon of crony capitalists for a breed of entrepreneurs who knew how to bend the rules to grow fast.

By mid 2000s, global private capital started making inroads into India. This, along with money from wealthy Indians, started becoming an option for Indian entrepreneurs looking for growth. Broadly, these funds can be classified as:

Angels: Wealthy individuals and funds ready to bet on a business idea of an entrepreneur. The risk appetite here is super high and money is used to convert an idea into a business. Investments normally happens at a seed or early stage allowing the angels to value the company low and take a large stake. Aarin Capital is an angel fund.

Venture Capital: These firms raise funds from limited partners who are generally deep-pocket investors like institutions, university endowments, super high-net-worth individuals, family offices, etc. They normally come in at the growth stage, i.e., after the company has proved the business through a minimum viable product (MVP) and is ready for big growth. They are differentiated from regular financial investors by actively providing operational guidance and scaling support. These funds are known to maintain operators as employees who then provide the investing organizations with functional expertise in key growth areas like branding, PR, technology, hiring, etc. Firms like Sequoia Capital, Accel Partners, Tiger Global and SoftBank fall under this category.

Private Equity: Super big money managers who are interested in investing in late stages after the business has stabilized, i.e., after the model is proven and risk is lower. Typically, these are extremely return on investment (RoI)-focused money managers who look at an enterprise from the lens of profit and loss (P&L). Normally, they are not interested in operations or understanding the business and prefer to focus on business metrics alone. The biggest names in the PE world are Blackstone, Kohlberg Kravis Roberts & Co., General Atlantic, etc.

Public Market Funds and Hedge Funds: The experts in stock markets and the ones who invest the money of pension funds, endowment funds, sovereign funds, mutual funds, asset management funds, etc. Their risk appetite is negligible, and they will invest typically closer to an initial public offering (IPO). Extremely good at spotting opportunities and making a killing. Funds like Blackrock Advisors, UBS and Silver Lake fall in this category.

As you can see, each of these funds specializes in investing in companies which are at a particular stage or stages in their growth journey.

Ripples of Quantitative Easing

From the investor perspective, start-ups are classified into three stages: seed/early stage, growth stage, late stage.

An early-stage investor specializes in investing in ideas and the entrepreneur and helps them in converting their passion into a business. Known in the investment and start-up world as angels, these companies deploy high-risk capital and can come in at very low valuations and get a large stake in the organization. Aarin was a seed/early-stage investor who literally found Byju the entrepreneur in Byju the teacher.

When a start-up reaches a particular scale and needs money for high growth, the second category of investors who specialize in growth capital starts pitching in. Informally known in India as VCs, thanks to the highly successful growth deals done by VCs like Sequoia Capital, Accel Ventures and Tiger Capital, these investors believe in coming in just before the hockey stick growth curve and supporting companies with both capital and their own strategic and operating resources.

It is at this stage that start-ups start seeing multi-million valuations and begin getting substantial money for scaling nationally. Since such deals in the private market were limited in India, these also resulted in high-visibility PR for these companies and investors. The growth stage of start-ups is also typically associated with high burn, i.e., the difference in their spendings and earnings in a fixed time period (could be a month, quarter or annual). This value typically is high and hence called burn because in a lot of cases they lose money faster than literally putting the cash on fire.

A late-stage investor comes onboard after the start-up has stabilized on both growth and burn; in other words, the business model is proven and predictable. The start-ups typically are close to profitability by then and have stable growth and margins. The risk associated with these investments are lower and hence the return more assured. The game here is highly dependent on how well one can source deals and have the credibility and cash to get in just before the public market debut.

An unwritten strategy employed by all these investors at every stage is that they specialize in finding the next-stage investor. A seed fund knows every growth-stage investor and actively pitches their investments to these funds from the moment it invests and sees business taking shape. The same is true with growth funds that act as an important source of information for late-stage investors on their deals. It's a close-knit industry and word travels fast here.

The Aarin investment brought Byju into this investor circle and the company started getting tracked by growth-stage funds. Mid 2014–15 was also a time of valuation exuberance in India. This phenomenon should be understood from a global perspective. Let's refer to our Fed rate chart again.

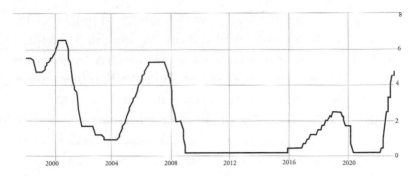

Fed rates 1995–2023

Tradingeconomics.com | Federal Reserve

Post the Lehman crash of 2008, the US emerged out of a long recession, with growth still looking wobbly. The Fed was supporting growth and recovery with near-zero interest rates since 2009. When low interest rates were not helping, they started using a non-traditional monetary policy known as quantitative easing to increase money supply in the market which could then be used to kick-start an investment cycle. Quantitative easing is basically Fed directly buying government and other securities and thus flooding the market with money. So, for a long period of time (2009–17), cheap money was available to US businesses and funds, but assets with good returns were limited. Globally, the Euro zone had crashed with a growth of 0.2 per cent and oil prices had plummeted. The Middle East was fighting the Islamic State of Iraq and the Levant (ISIS), protests had erupted in Hong Kong for democracy and Russia had just annexed Crimea. Narendra Modi got elected as the prime minister of India in 2014 with a thumping majority and was poised to take the country out of policy paralysis. Indian currency had fallen by as much as 40 per cent against the US dollar in the past eighteen months, and India under Modi was suddenly a great place to invest all the cheap money from developed economies in.

Flipkart, which struggled with a down round in 2012, saw its valuation go up by almost fifteen times to $11 billion in 2014–15. The entry of late-stage investors like hedge funds and sovereign funds looking for inflation-fighting returns for their money had changed the game for VCs. There was suddenly a lot of focus on finding entrepreneurs in new sectors which would grow, like e-commerce and Flipkart in India. The word 'tech' began appearing at the end of traditional business sectors to showcase how these were getting disrupted into high-growth businesses with the application of technology. While Paytm was the front runner in fintech, Ola was leading the cab aggregation, Swiggy just created the food-tech delivery which forced Zomato, a restaurant-review platform, to pivot into the same category. Money was finding visionary entrepreneurs with the help of angels. Edtech at that point was led by a company called Toppr, which created personalized assessments for kids to improve their learning. However, who will win the market was not clear and so VCs continued their search for more entrepreneurs; Byju was bang there at the right place and at the right time.

TV and Mobile Phone

'Nobody likes to take tests. No student will ever ask his parent to buy him an app for taking tests,' Byju told me on Toppr's business model. Unlike most entrepreneurs, Byju had a clear thesis and an MVP thanks to the investment he had been doing for years. And therefore, for Sequoia Capital, Byju sounded like a great bet—experienced, energetic and a visionary entrepreneur; a product ready to take off and a loyal and experienced team except for a few gaps they saw. They really saw the storyteller-founder who had not only seen good times but also had several scars from the bad times and understood that he could build truly remarkable things. By 2014, Sequoia had firmed up the investment decision and asked Byju to beef up his team with the next layer of leadership especially on the tech and consumer marketing side. On tech and product, Sequoia helped hiring senior leadership and, on the marketing side, Byju called me and asked me to join full time. It was truly a remarkable opportunity—to build the first global edtech brand from India which would become a household name in two to three years or at least that was the job description he gave me when he asked me to join.

From the beginning, Byju had a clear idea on how to build the brand. 'Biggest of the brands in India are built on TV. Work on a TV ad. That will bring growth,' he told me. 'Sir, TV is the route to build a national brand, I agree, and it is not only an expensive proposition but also a spray and pray approach. In Titan, the company only went on TV after establishing a distribution network across the country. The media buying was always done only in locations where the penetration was good. Else you will generate demand that can't be serviced, creating bad consumer experience.' I explained. 'But we are digitally distributed and sold. That's the beauty of it and hence we will cover the distance of a conventional brand in one-hundredth the time. I want to spend Rs 100 crore and capture the market before anyone else gets there.' He was right—BYJU'S, the learning app, the name of the app we had just launched, had classes from VI to XII in CBSE syllabus and enough content to have a pan-Indian appeal. The business model was to generate leads through online ads and then get our sales team to call these customers and sell them a paid subscription.

Since the product was online, we intuitively started acquiring customers online through digital marketing campaigns. Considering there were so few edtech players in the market, I had expected the cost per lead to be low due to lack of competition. I was wrong. Every coaching centre—local and national—was bidding for digital ad space and driving up prices. Since they were selling at higher price points, they could easily afford the high price but not us. Our sales model was not helpful either. Conversion on leads to payment were super low in the calling model since the parents were completely new to an online learning model and most of the time didn't even know their kid had put in a lead for a product like this. Most of these people saw us as spam and the process was painful. My thought was that even with a targeted and filtered approach, we are having so much of wastage of resources; a non-targeted medium like TV will give us super trash leads and the sales team will suffer. So, we were conflicted between two thought processes—we knew that the biggest of brands are built on TV while all the secondary data showed going on TV was not a prudent move for a digital brand. My experience in marketing had taught me that things don't always work as per secondary data. After all, if you torture data enough, it will tell you what you want to hear! So, I decided to pose my questions to people who had answers to every business problem—the customer.

Even in the early days, BYJU'S marketing was cutting edge and we were able to think big. Along with the audacious vision of the entrepreneur, this was helped by the hand-holding approach used by Sequoia with its start-ups. The firm employed one of the best marketers in India at that point— Raja Ganapathy—as the chief marketing officer, who along with his team, was involved in every step of our marketing scale-up, providing us with the guidance and opening doors for us. Raja had specialists in his team for media buying, PR, etc., and access to a whole lot of marketing research, thus helping us get the best rates and data when we started our brand marketing journey. In the next few weeks, we commissioned multiple customer visits and conducted in-depth interviews to better understand our target customer—kids and parents from middle-class aspirational families. Aspiration and education go hand in hand in India, with the latter seen as the only way to prosperity for the next generation of a middle-class family. This was our target group (TG). The visits and interviews confirmed a few things we already knew.

- The decision on any investment in education is appreciated and the parents will go to any level to make it happen if the kid wants the same.
- The decision is taken together, and the stakeholder set is complex with both parents and the kid having the veto power.
- At times, there are influencers like an elder brother or sister or a tuition teacher or even the patriarch of the family involved, who most of the time give their opinion basis limited knowledge but with an air of authority.

But the most interesting thing we noticed during these visits was the influence of media on their lives and the interplay between the TV and mobile phone. Households normally had a single TV set installed in the living room which became the focal point around which the family congregated during prime time. The programmes were usually of interest to the adults, but the kids were around too. Why? Because this was the time the kids got access to their favourite gadget—their father's mobile, the only computing device at home at that time. These were the pre-Jio days and largely households had just one mobile phone. The parents worried about the negative influence a mobile phone could have on their children and insisted they used the phone in front of them, forcing them to sit for the *saas-bahu* serials, accessing the world of internet through the slow 2G connection. We saw this behaviour repeat in smaller towns and were fascinated by what we saw. It gave us an interesting idea to bring together TV- and digital-lead generation.

Armed with a plethora of insights, our agency started working on the brand film. Since the stakeholder map included both parents and kids, the ad needed to speak to both. Such films are complex to implement in thirty to forty seconds especially when the value proposition the stakeholders are looking for can be conflicting. Add to it, the fact that the film should be clutter breaking. Considering this was our first film and of a virtually unknown brand, we decided to begin with a small shock to the viewers which would ensure their undivided attention for the next thirty seconds. I told them not to make it too cheesy, to which the agency responded saying that the TG likes it cheesy. I left it there since they were the experts. We then made the decision to keep the tag 'Fall in love with learning' and the call to action simple and measurable. Hence, just one message at the end of every single ad whichever medium it was run on—download the app for free! This was a monumental decision in the brand journey of BYJU'S; something we kept using without any changes for the next several years. This consistency in messaging was one of the main reasons why the brand was able to incrementally grow with every campaign without re-educating the customers.

Fall in Love with Learning

An agency will never let you read the script they have written. Because if you read it without the drama, it's never going to be approved. 'The ad will start with shots of students speaking about love. They will talk about how it was love at first sight, how they hated each other and then fell in love, how he is not too young to fall in love, etc. Most parents know that kids start these things in class by the time they are in standards VI and VII. However, talking about such things is a stigma and hence making such statements on TV will get the attention of everyone—parents because they are shocked and kids because they are curious where this is going. Then the ad will move on, and the kids will say that they are in love with the subjects they learn—math, physics, chemistry. The ad will go on to explain how with movie-like videos and smart assessments, BYJU'S, the learning app, will make learning enjoyable and fun, ending with our tag line—fall in love with learning,' the agency executive finished his dramatic narration and waited for feedback. Byju spoke first: 'We need a product window where we showcase how we teach. Else a customer will never be able to comprehend the richness of our product.' 'He is the CEO; he will get what he wants,' I thought. 'He is right. This is a new product with no precedent. How in the world is anyone going to visualize what we have created when we just say movie-like videos. It has been to in the face and shown to them.' After multiple debates and rewrites, our ad was finally ready. The agency head and the marketing team pushed hard not to have the product window which in their view was spoiling the story. However, Byju was firm—the product window had to be there and to ensure it didn't reduce the quality, he offered to record it himself using one of the most popular visualization techniques he had developed to teach the Pythagorean theorem. Another decision that helped our RoI in a big way.

The ad was cheesy in my view, but then our trials showed that the kids loved the film, so the agency knew what they were doing. Because of the way it began, the ad caught the attention of both parents and kids who watched. We obviously gave the kids the impression that this is a product which understands their generation and makes life easy for them in a way their parents may not understand or like. This made them interested in the product and they moved seamlessly to the next step of downloading the app. We took care that our media-buying mostly happened for prime time when we saw our TG sitting around the TV while the kids were on the mobile. Since the children were already sitting with the parents' mobile, the TV exposure immediately led to downloads. It didn't stop there: due to the uniqueness of the product and the first-mover advantage, the next day, the kids who had downloaded the app spoke about it in class to their friends, resulting in more downloads. The TV campaign ended up generating relevant leads for us at less than one-tenth the cost of generating a digital marketing lead. Interestingly, the customers were much more engaged than those of digital marketing leads since in the case of TV, they had had the opportunity to hear the story in the ad and experience the app before talking to our sales team.

The TV campaign solved the lead quantity and cost problem but didn't really improve the conversion issue drastically. In customer calls, I could clearly hear that they liked the product, but trust was still low to permit them to spend months of their salary. I could see this as a problem of idea sale rather than product sale since online learning was so new to Indians then. To solve this end to end, I started focusing on the full funnel, i.e., changes in the sales process, post generation of the lead. Thus started our pivots of the sales process to reach that sweet spot which would help us build a sustainable business.

First, we focused a lot on training, productizing the sales process as much as possible. For instance, there were separate pitches on how you should talk to the parent or the student depending on who is picking up the call. Since the decision-maker was usually a parent, the focus was to talk to them after taking the student into confidence about the pitch. At that point, we used to ship our paid product as content burned on to SD cards to customers who have made the payment. This was a rather unconventional way of shipping for a digital company; this decision was driven by the fact that internet speeds in India at that point were not good enough for streaming our high-definition videos. So, to ensure that the experience was good, we shipped an SD card which could be inserted into a mobile phone or tab and played using the BYJU'S app.

Soon we realized that even this approach didn't make sense since the kid didn't have access to the only mobile device at home, i.e., the father's mobile when the kid wanted to study. So, we started shipping a preloaded tablet. We debated if we should lock the tab and decided against it because kids were infatuated about owning their own devices and were not happy to know they could only study with those tabs. Hence locking was given as an option to the parent, and we left it to the kids to convince them.

Our sales team, meanwhile, started using tablets to excite the students to upgrade the freemium subscription to paid. The mechanism was no different from certain colleges giving a laptop during admissions and it worked well in India. It played on the weird prejudice of us Indians, who believed that such devices would distract and spoil the kid. The price is also a detractor; most of us believed it makes no sense paying so much for something which is just entertainment—an expensive toy. However, the moment you bundle it with education, all biases disappear. Even pricing is not a deterrent because education is an investment, and nothing will be held back. However, kids don't have such prejudices. They know the joy of internet and aspire to have a device to go online. It's true that a lot of time is wasted consuming entertainment and playing games, but that anyway is the case without a tab, laptop or internet. 'Every generation feels that the next generation is lazy and time has proved that with every new generation, we have only gotten smarter and efficient. It's a problem of perspective leading to ignorance. Our parents didn't grow up using computers and have hardly used the internet. They just don't understand this new generation which grew up online.' That was Byju typically bending reality with his pitch, and from a stratospheric view, it even made sense. 'Even teaching kids to write doesn't make sense any more. Who will write in the next generation? People will only type and use narration software,' he continued. When I didn't have an answer, it was Pravin—one of Byju's students who has been part of the company's journey from day one who responded: 'Writing is an important skill, and everyone should learn to write. Lot of people understand better by writing what they have heard. We can't take such a stance for now.' He closed the discussion with a smile.

As someone who held the prejudice myself, I was uncomfortable with the approach of disproportionately selling on the tab rather than on the beautiful learning product we had built. It was comprehensive and easily the best available anywhere in the world. Vinay, ably supported by Prakash, the new chief technology officer who joined with the help of Sequoia, had improved the product substantially with multiple engagement tools. The product journeys now helped the kids with 'how to learn' and not just 'what to learn'. Product journeys had its origins in the fact that some teachers can teach much better than others because of the way they have structured the content. They follow a logical order of delivery helping the student to easily navigate from one concept to another and ensure that prerequisites required to follow the chapter are dealt with before the chapter begins, without assuming that the student should already know all these. In other words, for these teachers, learning is a journey—starting with preparation and navigating with logic. Vinay and Prakash firmed up the journeys with multiple categories of questions, making it a joyous experience by using the latest development in tech and UI/UX. They even tried the viral 'swipe right-swipe left' user interface (UI) for true and false questions.

Another feature which came with journeys was personalization. Journeys allowed students to branch out into multiple pathways depending on their proficiency levels. The algorithm was able to detect the concept a student was weak in if a particular mistake was made and point the kid to the video of that concept, which would take the student to a different pathway and bring him back to the core journey after he proved to the algorithm that he had understood the concept. At that point, I had looked at multiple apps which claimed the same but couldn't find anything which came even close to our product. Quite predictably, the engagement hit the roof and now kids were actually spending a lot of time on the app exploring and learning immediately after download. This allowed our sales guys to have a good conversation with parents and kids on their current academic and learning levels and where they needed improvement. However, the disproportionate use of tab as the selling point still continued.

I saw it as a training issue and felt the sales team did not know our product well and hence was using the easy route of selling the tab. However, any amount of training didn't help, and kids were convincing their parents seeing the tabs. It was like that pull product and the sales guys obviously hung on

to the same USP to make things happen. To me, selling a tab
with content is what anyone can do and soon hordes of clones
followed like Extramarks and Eduisfun; some even using the
same model of tablet we sold. Interestingly, these products
couldn't impact our sales and actually helped improve our
positioning through comparison. Thanks to competition who
were selling tabs, our sales team was forced to pitch our product
features thus slowly moving away from a disproportionate focus
on the device. I justified the marketing strategy as a kickback to
students given by parents to study; that's a very normal thing in
our homes. We routinely got an hour of TV if we completed our
homework. Studying at home has been a negotiated barter for
long. Slowly conversion started improving but not at the pace
we were burning money, and stress started to build up again.

Chapter 5

Founders, Facebook and Fortitude

Fortitude is an important trait investors look for in entrepreneurs. Entrepreneur and venture capitalist Peter Thiel exemplifies this when he says, 'Brilliant thinking is rare, but courage is even [in] shorter supply than genius,' in his famous lectures on entrepreneurship at Stanford. While growing, the entrepreneur faces multiple adversities—small, big and terrible. However big the adversity, an entrepreneur can never give up. He cannot lose his cool, cannot panic and must fight it, and foray his organization to a new dawn. Byju epitomized this courage to fight all odds. For him, no problem is big enough to be a crisis, and I have never seen him panicking or taking pressure. It is this cool-headed approach that helped him resolve crisis after crisis. One such crisis was looming in mid-2016 when the growth run rate was not accelerating as expected, thus increasing burn.

By 2016, it was evident that whatever we were doing was working but not at the pace we had anticipated. Byju, hence, went on a high drive trying to raise more cash to thread the bridge. While he spoke to our existing investors for a bridge round (financing which would help the company tide over till the next investment round), he also started meeting prospective investors, including the CEO and vice chairman of Times Internet, Satyan Gajwani.

The Stanford-educated scion of the Bennett Coleman group is not only a successful CEO who is giving a new direction to the legacy print business of *Times of India* but also one of the most successful start-up investors in India today, with a knack for identifying entrepreneurs with calibre. He bought MX Player, then a lesser-known brand, for $140 million in 2018 and propelled it in the direction of ad-based free OTT business model. MX Player saw its series A valuation go up to $500 million in a year and during Covid-19 times, it was the largest OTT in India in terms of subscribers. There were talks of investments at $1 billion valuation in 2021 for the combined entity of MX Player and MX TakaTak. It is not surprising that the founder in Satyan saw a founder's fire in Byju and decided to do a deal with him. But it didn't end there. Seeing the unique digital model in education and the distance Byju had already traversed, Satyan did an introduction with the family office of Mark Zuckerberg, Facebook founder, and his wife Priscilla Chan. This was an unbelievable opportunity for an Indian start-up and the PR we could leverage from something like this was incredible. Byju knew this well and started planning for the meeting with Chan Zuckerberg Initiative (CZI).[6]

The opportunity finally came when Byju was on the way to the airport with his family for a trip to Kerala. He got a call asking if he could meet the founder of Facebook the next

6   Debarghya Sil, 'MX Player's FY22 Loss Nears $100 Mn Mark', 22 March 2023, https://inc42.com/buzz/mx-players-loss-widens-1-2x-in-fy22-nears-100-mn-mark/#:~:text=MX%20Player%2C%20which%20was%20initially,valuation%20of%20over%20%24500%20Mn.
    Jai Vardhan, 'Exclusive: MX Player likely to turn unicorn with over $100 Mn in fresh funding', https://entrackr.com/2021/03/exclusive-mx-player-likely-to-turn-unicorn-with-over-100-mn-in-fresh-funding/.

day in San Francisco. Without batting an eyelid, he said, 'I will be in SF tomorrow, will meet as per convenience.' Then he explained to his family the importance of this meeting and bought the fastest ticket to SF at the airport after sending his family to Kerala. Breaking his journey at multiple cities to find an earlier flight, he made it to SF in time and impressed the CZI team with the BYJU'S story.

CZI is a unique fund because they do both non-profit and for-profit investments in two domains which the Zuckerberg family is passionate about—education and health. The idea of BYJU'S sat well with the theme of CZI i.e., making a change in the world for better. BYJU'S by then had kids from more than a thousand towns learning from our content. We were offering an opportunity to millions of kids from small towns to learn with the highest quality of content, truly making education accessible. Add to it the aura of a truly home-conceptualized and home-grown product unlike an idea copied from what was working in the US or China; BYJU'S quickly started becoming an investor's favourite.

With all these investors now lined up, Byju was able to do our series B round at a much higher valuation. Valuation rounds are called series A, B, C, etc. because typically investors who come on board at various stages hold different rights and liquidation preferences. Though the same is not exactly true for most start-ups today, the series names stuck. For instance, BYJU'S didn't give investors any liquidity preferences.

While we were engaged in some serious marketing and brand building, we knew clearly that the mileage we were going to get for the Zuckerberg story would be massive. So, we planned the PR well. One of the things that came with CZI funding was a post by Zuckerberg on Facebook from his personal account announcing the thought behind the investment. This meant that in one shot, BYJU'S was going to be seen and read about by millions of the founder's followers. Most importantly, it came with the credibility of Zuckerberg and Facebook and hence would be celebrated world over.

The post hit the world on 8 September 2016 and quickly went viral. It hit the 50 million followers of Zuckerberg and got shared by thousands of people in India who took pride in the company. The post did more impressions and clicks than what Rs 10 crore of media money could have bought us on Facebook then. More importantly, the goodwill we got was priceless.

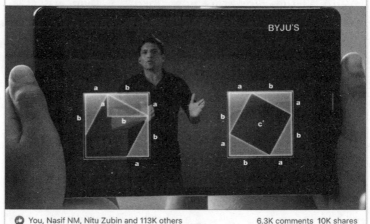

Mark Zuckerberg ✓
8 September 2016 · 🌐

As part of the Chan Zuckerberg Initiative, Priscilla and I are investing in an Indian education technology company we're excited about called BYJU's.

BYJU's was started by a teacher and entrepreneur named Byju Raveendran as a way to help students from different backgrounds across India learn in a way that works best for them. The mobile app uses a mix of video lessons and interactive tools to help teach subjects like math and science for a fraction of what other services cost. So far, BYJU's has 250,000 subscribers who use the app for an average of 40 minutes a day -- and it's working. A survey found that almost 80 percent of parents said it improved their children's learning dramatically.

I'm optimistic about personalized learning and the difference it can make for students everywhere. That's why it's a major focus of our education efforts, and why we're looking forward to working with companies like BYJU's to get these tools into the hands of more students and teachers around the world.

👍 You, Nasif NM, Nitu Zubin and 113K others   6.3K comments 10K shares

Zuckerberg's post on Facebook post investment
Source: Facebook

When I joined BYJU'S leaving TAS, my family found it tough to explain to people around them as to why their son left Tatas for an unknown and funny-sounding company. Of all the people, my sister was the angriest and refused to reveal the name of the new company I worked in. She kept telling her friends, 'He used to work in TAS' and limited my introduction to that. When Zuckerberg posted, I took a snapshot of the post and WhatsApp-ed it to her along with the post link saying, 'Now you can tell your friends I work for BYJU'S, the only company in Asia in which Mark Zuckerberg has invested.'

By the end of 2016, we were feeling good about ourselves. Our brand was surging ahead and had occupied a special place in our customer's mind. Our paid customers were super happy, and we were seeing an unprecedented 80 per cent-plus repeat purchase, an important metric for sustainable business. Our marketing spends were optimized and we suddenly became a brand people wanted to be associated with. However, the conversions were still nowhere close to where we wanted them to be. This was putting a lot of pressure on all of us and more burn. Byju knew that he couldn't keep raising money and the business needed to make money. For this, he was counting on us, and we were clueless. The business needed more ideas and like always, ideas finally came from my favourite people—the customers.

Chapter 6

Pay in Parts

I have always seen my parents pay my school fees term-wise. Even if paying full-year was possible, we Indians preferred term-wise since it made more sense cash flow-wise, and nobody was busy enough to mind making three trips to the school in a year. Fundamentally, we are a savings-focused society and for us every penny counts. The schools also never gave a discount for paying the full annual fees in one go because it made no sense to do the same for an enterprise which was non-profit as per regulation. It is only recently that some new-generation schools have introduced discounts for paying full-year fees. Thanks to this well-established practice, we are still used to paying for education in instalments. A lot might have changed in all our lives, but the practice of paying for education in instalments is something ingrained in our psyche. Or at least I thought so.

This is where the first of the two big ideas which would change the course of the organization came from—zero-cost EMIs or instalments. I kept hearing the request for instalments again and again while listening to calls from customers which didn't get converted. Instalments have been an inherent part of the education system in India. Since BYJU'S was an educational product, the customer was expecting to pay for it in instalments. Instalments also cannot come at an extra cost. At an extra cost, it gets perceived as a loan and taking a loan for supplementary education is not something customers preferred.

The idea sprang to life when Bajaj Finserv came to pitch their zero-cost EMI product. The solution allowed holders of Bajaj cards with an approved line of credit to buy products and pay back in six, nine or twelve EMIs. These EMIs or instalments were at zero cost, i.e., no interest was charged to the customers. Bajaj made money by charging a subvention to brands like us who wanted to give this facility to our customers. I could see that Bajaj could solve our problem of instalments, but the issue was that the entire process of buying using the credit line existed only offline and nobody had till then found a reason to do it online. As a financing option, Bajaj was used mostly for white-goods purchases in electronics stores.

With our calling-based sales model, we never met our customers physically and hence we needed an online version of the same buying process. Luckily, Suneesh, the person pitching the model to me from Bajaj, was my batchmate from NITC. Suneesh was as passionate about the project as I was about cracking instalments and was willing to pitch this idea to the Bajaj product team and create a mechanism in return for the new business it could potentially generate for Bajaj Finserv. Thus, Suneesh and I sat together and designed the first-ever one-time password-based instalment process in education which he then pitched to his risk team. Luckily, Bajaj saw the potential of doing the process completely online and was ready to experiment the same with us. We soon launched the facility to pay the fees in monthly instalments of six, nine or twelve, to Bajaj customers who were buying BYJU'S. With this, our customers had an option to pay Rs 2000 monthly and buy our Rs 24,000 tablet if they had a Bajaj EMI card. Bajaj active cardholders at that time numbered around 7 million and the base had good intersection with our customers. This changed things greatly and a large part of our customer base started feeling that our product was indeed affordable. The value proposition of one year of comprehensive math and science learning and a tab for just Rs 2000 per month was appealing to even middle-class parents in small towns. The uptick was substantial and finally I saw the unit economics moving towards positivity. However, this was just the beginning. If the first idea of the two helped us scale well, it was the second one which made us a juggernaut.

Field Sales

While our experiments solved quite a few problems in conversion, trust issue was not something we could solve yet. Calls after calls, I could hear people hang up because they didn't trust the unknown guy at the other end calling them out of the blue and telling them about some new company which will teach their kids better and charge Rs 24,000, that too using a tab. Sounds like a scam!

Our brainstorming sessions were around bridging this chasm of trust. We looked at various companies which had scaled pan-India from education to telecom and we saw a pattern—face-to-face interaction. While scaling a new product across the length and breadth of the country, successful brands had to rely on meeting their customers face to face. To make this happen, they established partners or offices in hundreds of cities and towns. Even companies selling telephony couldn't close sales over the telephone after a point; they set up retail stores and asked customers to walk in and experience the brand and service.

Taking a leaf out of that playbook, our experimentation moved towards making face-to-face interaction with customers happen. This presented new challenges. With the national marketing campaigns, we were generating leads from across the country and hence counsellors used to get leads from towns hundreds of kilometres apart, making physical meetings impossible. So, first pilots were to try to do Skype calls (a bit unwieldy now that we have better video calling service providers) with the customers and try conversions by pitching the product on a video call. We quickly realized that the technological challenges made this impossible. A small minority of our customers had a device and good internet connection at home to instal the app and get on a Skype call. The idea hence was a non-starter. So, the trials moved towards seeing if the counsellor could go and visit the customer and close the sale. This required some major changes in the way we assigned and organized our sales teams. We would have to begin giving leads of a particular city and its neighbouring areas to a set of sales guys who would then meet the customers to convert sales rather than trying it on phone.

Typically, companies, like banks, do this kind of sales with a two-layered sales organization. The first set of callers is employed to break the ice and fix an appointment for the sales staff who are on field. The field staff distributed across the city then go and meet the customers at the appointed time slots and close the sales. We found the regular model an overkill and decided to use the same person for fixing appointments and home visits. We could clearly see that the field sales would only work when parents and kids were together at home which meant we only had a few slots: over weekends and late evenings, if the parents agreed to it. This meant the sales guys were free on weekdays during which they could make the appointment calls. We ran several pilots with this model in the top cities of Bengaluru, NCR and Mumbai to understand the right process and kept improving the process till we saw ten times conversions vs calling model.

'Our field sales are working very well, but it only covers the four cities where we have offices. We are missing out on vast parts of upcountry towns and worst, we are losing tons of leads which come from these places,' Divya told us in one of our catch ups. 'We don't have enough lead base to set up so many offices. Will have to figure out a new sales model for this. Something of a hub and spoke model,' I replied. 'Why don't we have the lead base to set up offices everywhere? Why can't we increase marketing and double up the new brand campaign. It seems to be doing well,' Byju chipped in. We had just launched our new brand campaign where we built further on the last message of 'fall in love with learning'. This time, the ad showcased parents spying on their children while they were on the phone. The earlier generation always felt the device was for entertainment purposes alone and was a cause for distraction during studies. The kids showed them that they were actually studying using BYJU'S and that this is the new way to learn. The premise again tried to highlight the biases against technology and bundle education with it. We believed deeply that the traditional medium of learning, i.e., textbooks, evolved in an era when visuals couldn't be stored and reproduced cheaply, and hence text became the default way of disseminating knowledge. Today, thanks to cheap computing power, visuals—alongside text and audio—which make learning much more fun and engaging is cheap to produce and consume. Consequently, there is no need to be stuck in the textual way of learning. It's time to change the medium of learning from books to tablets!

The statistics of our ad engagement showed that we were making huge progress in terms of moving the needle in this conversation, with our fun ads. Along with our field sales experiments, we were now converting leads at a good pace, which were getting generated from these campaigns. However, Byju, seeing the opportunity, wanted to do much more. While my mind was fixated on the idea of creating a hub-and-spoke model, Byju was plotting an explosive expansion across the country. While I could manage to rely on my team to crack the hub-and-spoke model, he needed a brand ambassador who could give us credibility overnight pan-India, and Byju already had someone in mind.

Chapter 7

The Math Musical

In brand marketing, a brand goes through multiple stages in its journey: awareness, consideration, conversion.

The route is typically true of an Indian brand which is priced above the impulse price range. In the awareness phase, the customers who are part of the TG of the brand are exposed to the brand. The few interactions with the brand message make them aware of the brand and the brand promise. When Air Deccan wanted to create awareness of its low-cost flights which almost anyone could afford, it built a 150-second ad famous as 'Old man and the sky'. The ad shows a villager taking his first flight, booked by his son. The heart-warming ad thus positions the airline as helping the average Indian fly. Though the ad created awareness of the product, it took a lot more time for the average start considering air travel as an option.

In the next phase, customers who were now aware were given more information on how the brand will help their lives. This deeper knowledge builds consideration for product purchase. Flipkart's 'No kidding. No worries' campaign, in which grown-ups were replaced by kids, was aimed at increasing consideration. The kids discuss purchase decision by talking about the features Flipkart offers, like a thirty-day replacement, variety, etc. Each of these features were meant to convince the customers already aware of brand Flipkart that this is a great proposition.

In the final phase, the conversion or the sales starts happening automatically since the product is proven and its application well established. Typically, the process takes tens of years to become a conversion brand pan-India even with loads of investment. A full-page ad by JioMart with discounts on hundreds of products is created for conversion or sales alone from a brand which is well established.

For a product like BYJU'S, this expansion needed a lot of product changes like creating the same product in local languages. Byju aspired to cover this journey in record time, something which quite a few well-invested digital-first brands of India in the 2010s were trying to do. Flipkart and Paytm were demonstrating the same to some extent, but what Byju had in mind was something much bigger and faster than that.

'Why can't we get Shah Rukh Khan [SRK] as our brand ambassador? He has the fan following and credibility needed to give us leads from every nook and corner of the country. We can expand the teams across and really grow the market and the revenue,' Byju asked us all. 'I don't think we are ready for celebrity endorsement yet. A face like SRK will explode our traffic and bring in lakhs of unqualified leads. Our nascent field sales conversion model, which is giving good results, will go for a toss. We have just proved our hub-and-spoke model and are in the early days of expanding teams across tier-2 markets. This will stress the entire system and break it. We should build incrementally, and our last film is working well. Let it run its course,' I responded immediately. To which Byju replied, 'That's a very tentative way of doing things and I don't do anything tentatively. Our business model is working, and I want to go all out. A celebrity will give us instant credibility across the country. You guys should scale the field sales and hub-and-spoke model across the country by then. Take the sales team strength to 3000 people immediately and set up offices in all key locations. With the hub-and-spoke model, we will then be able to cover the entire country from these offices. We have gone to towns where we knew no one or their language and still managed to conduct mega events with 1000 attendees in a week's time. You should be able to build the office network and hire people in three months.'

I was ruminating on the challenge when I heard someone else in the group ask the next question: 'Why SRK? The generation of students who uses our product follow people like Justin Bieber and Ranbir Kapoor. Are you sure film stars are good representatives for an education product?' The question came from our advisor and hence was taken seriously. Byju explained, 'The next ad will be about credibility and trust building and not just the early awareness. We are already popular among the student population. It's the parents who should now start looking at us as a trustworthy company. So, we need someone that generation admires and trusts.' 'Why not Amitabh Bachchan, then, or Aamir Khan? Aamir may be a perfect fit; he even played a teacher in his recent hit *Taare Zameen Par*.' It was a pointed response to the not-so-clear reason presented by Byju. 'I think AB has worked for some education brand and Aamir is too niche,' Byju responded. When the entrepreneur has made up his mind, everyone else falls in line; that's how it works! There is a reason for it—the entrepreneur has built the enterprise almost single-handedly and knows the pulse of his audience. He may not always be able to articulate the same and hence everyone prefers to fall in line.

I could see how SRK could be a great fit. First, he is a doting father; an image he has built over time. Second, he has a pan-Indian popularity especially in the generation of the parents of our students and third, he had huge digital presence unlike any other actor. All this in my opinion made him a great choice for BYJU'S. However, I was still sceptical about our ability to build a distribution good enough to leverage the impact an SRK ad will create. Moreover, I was also worried about the overshadowing impact SRK could have on our young brand.

Experienced marketers don't launch their brand with a celebrity. The celebrity who is already very famous gives the brand a lot of eyeballs but also end up making the brand forever associated and subservient to himself or herself. This association will forever make the brand a second fiddle to the celebrity thus not giving it an opportunity to make an impact with its customer or occupy a unique space in the minds of its customers. This is what happened with brands like AskMe. com-Super App (launched with Ranbir Kapoor) as the 'Baap of all pay apps', Eduauraa-Edtech app (launched by Ranveer Singh). These brands spent tens of crores on their launch or early marketing with celebrities and ended up getting completely eclipsed. Raja and team from Lowe Lintas also gave the same assessment and hence the fact that the brand should not get eclipsed by the celebrity was an important condition in our campaign brief. It may sound nuts—paying crores to get a celebrity for the ad and then writing a film where he is just 30 per cent of the film. But that's exactly the point—marketing is never obvious and the best outcomes are delivered when you think ahead and not react based on your first instinct.

This was also the time when Amazon was fast capturing the Indian market with their excellent products, services and marketing. Their jingle-based ad film was capturing the imagination of the country. Jingles have always fascinated me; I felt that for a country like India where we have grown up listening to so much music right from the suprabhatham we wake up to, it's a fantastic vehicle for virality especially if one is using TV as a medium. Hence, I requested the agency for two things: to make the film jingle based and to see if you can connect it with what SRK is known for and use one of their cheeky ways to connect it back to education.

The agency started with the 'impossible' task of delivering a film which covered all these aspects and would be acceptable to the superstar too. After several rewrites, we finalized on a script where students would perform a dance on a song made up of math formulas and SRK would be the master of the ceremony introducing the piece to the audience, which comprised parents. In a nice twist of wordings, they connected our tag line 'Fall in love with learning' to the lover-boy image of SRK. Byju didn't spare any expenditure in the production of the ad film which came out as one of the best I have ever seen. When he saw it for the first time, Byju exclaimed, 'This is a math musical. Excellent ad! We will rock it.'

While all this marketing work was happening, our sales team was working round the clock building distribution which could leverage SRK. We worked on weekends interviewing and hiring people, and weekdays in driving sales and setting up new teams and offices. We travelled the length and breadth of the country establishing offices and onboarding team members. In a short span of three months, BYJU'S sales organization and offices grew five-fold, covering almost the entire country. Again, taking a cue from an idea given by Byju, we were able to convince multiple employees working in our calling team in the city offices to move to their respective cities and join the offices set up in those cities. These employees who were well trained in our products and processes provided the critical link and helped us get the teams up and running quickly. Much faster than we could imagine.

The SRK ad was launched with a bang. We first launched it on YouTube and the big screens of PVR. The ad garnered 5,00,000 views in one night on YouTube and had multiple people sharing it both online and as social posts after seeing it before the movie screening at PVR. Some elite individuals shared posts about our ad, calling the ad cringe-worthy and saying how we were wasting money for education on celebrity endorsement. A great advertisement polarizes the audience to a certain extent. This is just a reflection of how different audiences are and has nothing to do with anyone being right or wrong.

Some of the best marketers I had worked with in Fastrack used to leverage this insight in a rather interesting way. Whenever they made an ad for Fastrack, the young Fastrack team would love it and the senior employees, who were part of the Titan top management, would be scandalized. It was the latter response that the team sought. I had a similar feeling seeing comments in social media by these elitists.

The first SRK campaign was the most successful campaign ever in the history of the brand BYJU'S. Before the campaign and through it as well, we built a pan-India distribution network with sixty-plus offices and 3000-plus sales counsellors meeting the customers SRK and the kids were enticing with our math musical. The Baazigar had clearly worked his *jadoo* on our customers and got the money registers ringing. Not all customers though—there were pockets in the country where he had limited influence; cracking those was another story!

Chapter 8

Going Local, Going Deep

The year 2018 was good for BYJU'S. Finally, all cylinders were firing, and revenue was flowing at the pace of investments. The record time in which BYJU'S set up distribution was a testimony to the nascent but fast-developing start-up ecosystem of the country. A lot of start-ups, like us, were foraying into the vast tier-2 and tier-3 markets and were leveraging each other for expansion. Our team members used Ola to travel and meet customers across the country and stayed at Oyo if the visit required an overnight stay. Pretty much all tools used by us were cloud-based and developed by budding start-ups—LeadSquared for customer relationship management, Ameyo for cloud telephony, Clevertap for messaging; the list went on and on. Even our EMI partner now was a new-age start-up—Capital Float (now Axio) run by two Stanford graduates. Capital Float developed a proprietary flow using Aadhaar to complete the entire loan-approval process at the customer's location without the need of a bank executive at site. Today, everyone uses a version of this innovation. Interestingly, all of us were making losses and surviving on the investor's money. So, in a way, these VCs were paying to make India's tier-2 and tier-3, and beyond, accessible as well as spreading prosperity.

How ironical would our founding socialist fathers find this if they had seen this day! Capitalism was doing what socialism couldn't achieve in sixty years of Independence—well almost.

Bollywood and SRK are popular across the country—from Gujarat to Arunachal and Kashmir to Kerala. However, in the prosperous southern states of Tamil Nadu, Kerala, Andhra Pradesh, Telangana and Karnataka, the popularity and reach of Tamil, Malayalam, Telugu and Kannada movies is much more than of Hindi movies. We could see this phenomenon in our numbers too. While there was a huge growth in our numbers and conversion in the Hindi heartlands, metros and tier-1 cities across the country including south India, growth in overall business in the South was not too impressive. This led us to the next stage of marketing—going deep in key markets.

'When it comes to education, each district in Kerala can have as many students as all of Bangalore. That's the potential of our tier-2 markets.' Byju set the strategy clearly: 'Southern states give much more importance to education than northern states, and we should now figure out how we can go deep into these states and make them each as big as fourteen Bangalores.' 'I agree. So far we have been going wide; now our focus should be to go deep,' I concurred. For a traditional organization, there is a sea difference between the two approaches. It could mean doing crores worth of capital investment establishing retail stores, hiring locals and innovating on unique distribution modes which work in the area they want to go deep in. But not with a digital-first company like BYJU'S. With a sales team which was already spread across the country and full of locals who could speak the local language, there wasn't much that needed to be done to change the approach. All the changes needed to happen in product and marketing.

BYJU'S products focused on CBSE and ICSE syllabuses and were recorded in English. Going deep into Kerala, Tamil Nadu, Andhra Pradesh, Telangana and Karnataka meant building on the syllabuses of these states and that too in their local languages. We researched our customers and non-customers in these states and dug deep to understand the product changes. Finally, we decided to make the product map on to various state syllabuses but not change the language from English to the local language. The finding was that English in India is seen as the language which prepares the child for success in the future and most parents aspire to give their kids English-medium education. Hence, the decision to map the product to various state syllabuses and but do the delivery in English. Initial product testing gave us good feedback and one more insight—parents wanted their kids to learn in English but their English was poor, and the pace at which our product was delivered, they hardly understood anything. So, we started working on new product features which would make the product more acceptable and effective in tier-2 India. We added subtitles in local languages and an option to slow down the pace of delivery.

In some languages, notably Hindi and Hinglish, where we saw potential, we translated the entire audio and added an option in the product to switch between English or Indian language at will. This was not a simple tech feature to build and it had the potential to completely change the access of education. Imagine giving a kid in Bhagalpur access to a lecture of a Nobel laureate Massachusetts Institute of Technology (MIT) professor at a click of a button which will translate the lecture into Maithili, his mother tongue. Kids across the country would be able to access the latest knowledge repositories.

On the marketing side, we crafted campaigns for the local audience by building on the learnings of using brand ambassador SRK. In place of SRK, we chose top movie stars from their respective states—Mohanlal in Malayalam and Mahesh Babu in Telugu—and recreated the same script and approach across languages. Our agency wrote a script which worked across the genre and the process was quite seamless. In Tamil, one of the biggest markets for us, we realized that Tamil movie stars, at least the big names, didn't promote brands any more. At that point, we would have spoken to several stars, only to hear a clear no coming from them.

The blitz marketing with local superstars alongside product localization and local media buys were successful, and business in southern Indian states started showing a big uptick. Along with all the marketing, the free PR we got due to our message of making quality education accessible and affordable to all acted as the force multiplier. Byju however was not happy and wanted to explore one more blitz idea. This was around India's so-called national religion—cricket.

Chapter 9

BYJU'S Bleeds Blue

Thanks to the popularity of cricket in India and the explosive growth triggered by the Indian Premier League (IPL), the cost of sporting properties went through the roof. Of all the properties, the official sponsorship of the Indian cricket team which comes with the chest branding of the team jersey is the most lucrative. Sahara was a brand that recognized the power and prestige of a spend like this very early on. They leveraged it so well that an unknown private finance company headquartered in Lucknow was able to metamorphosize into a multinational conglomerate which ran an airline and bought luxury properties in London and New York.

It's interesting to see the history of brands who sponsored this space. For ten years each, the space was sponsored by one of India's largest cigarette brands Wills and a little-known finance company Sahara. Post that came Star TV for some few years. Star backed off when the Chinese mobile maker Oppo bought it for a princely sum of Rs 1079 crore for five years. One needs a very large margin like cigarettes or a mysterious business model like Sahara to afford the jersey, and the mobile phone maker soon realized this. In two-and-a-half years, they were negotiating their way out of the deal.[7]

It is Byju's love for sports that got the brand close to sports sponsorships. The RoI from sports properties during the awareness-building phase was stellar and we continued picking up associations in the form of ad spots, associate sponsorships and even title sponsorships. From the initial days itself, the RoIs on sports properties were always good and had developed gigantic ambitions. We had at length, thought through the possibilities like the Board of Control for Cricket in India (BCCI), Barcelona FC (Byju's favourite football club and where his icon Messi played), Manchester United FC and Indian cricket team sponsorships. So, when two separate agents reached out to both Byju and me with the Oppo development, they were speaking to prepared minds.

'If it was Barcelona, I would not have thought twice but the price paid by Oppo for the Indian cricket jersey is too high to make any business sense,' Byju told me over the phone. It was 2 a.m. for me in Palo Alto and the frantic call from the agent woke me up. I was handling the international business by then and was just a sounding board for him. 'The Indian cricket jersey is a unique advertising property and I think we have reached a stage in our brand journey where we can pull off a name branding. It sure is expensive and Oppo seems desperate, so I know you will negotiate till the last dime. That's a given,' I responded. 'Yes, that I'm doing and I'm doing it myself so that we get the best price. Do you think

---

7   PTI, 'BYJU's to replace Oppo on Team India jersey', *Sportstar*, 25 July 2019, https://sportstar.thehindu.com/cricket/oppo-to-be-replaced-by-byjus-on-indian-cricket-team-jersey/article28706334.ece

it's worth it?' he enquired. Byju was in one of his moments before the big win; he always is in this thinking-taking input state just before he goes on stage to create a big blast of a session. I could sense that it was such a moment. 'Sir, I think it's worth it if you can close below the rate we had derived in our analysis. There are enough matches with big teams and I think the fact that an education company is sponsoring our cricket team, which carries so many hopes and expectations of the nation, will be big news. The team has carried the burden of tobacco, deposit schemes, real estate, Chinese mobiles, etc., for long; it's time to associate it with nation-building,' I could feel myself getting excited when I responded to him and hoped we would embellish the famous blue jersey. He laughed and told me he would try his best, but he would not do a deal that would bleed us. Byju the ace negotiator took over then on.

In a couple of weeks, the nation woke up to the news of BYJU'S sponsoring the Indian cricket team. It was a huge win for a start-up which was virtually unknown a couple of years back. Now it was a household name. Rarely does a brand achieve such a feat in a complex nation like India. While patriotism and nationalism were the undertones we wanted to ride on with our sponsorship of the Indian team, the whole display got a boost due the way the brand name BYJU'S was highlighted on the jersey. It literally read 'BYJU'S India'. The picture reminded our investors of the audacity Byju had in putting his name on the company. Here again, it was as if he was taking responsibility of the team by calling it BYJU'S. 'I hope they will win matches after so much of BYJU'S training,' an investor quipped after seeing the new jersey.

The BCCI sponsorship was a comprehensive one which covered Men's, Women's and Under-19 teams. BYJU'S also ended up making the best of the women's cricket team sponsorship riding on the rising popularity of the format delivering disproportionate RoI on that investment. The same cannot be said assertively about the main jersey sponsorship. From an attributable RoI perspective, it is a complex investment to measure and if one tries conventional ways of measurement, you would end up thinking it was a bleeding investment. After all, SRK has ensured that BYJU'S App and love for learning were known to most Indians, so why did you need the Indian cricket team to say the same?

However, conventional tools are not really the right way to measure such monumental cultural events. The unattributable brand rub-off can have a much larger impact and it's impossible to measure the trust, credibility and association with a champion that the association with the Indian cricket team would have brought.

With the growth in brand, larger marketing investments started yielding lower returns on investment. While this cannot be easily ascertained for brand spends, this can be easily seen on performance marketing investments. Increasingly, I felt that we had surpassed the stage of awareness and it was time to be razor-focused on consideration and conversion. The phase called for ruthless cutting down of marketing spends and relooking the entire sales and marketing channels. The RoI was not the only reason which made me feel it was time to change our approach, there were other glaring aspects too.

Chapter 10

Waves of Indian Edtech

All the blitz marketing one does brings a lot of aura to the brand. Not only do you become attractive to your customers and investors but also to competitors and companies operating in adjacencies. Especially companies operating in adjacent segments of the sector like school edtech start getting interested in associating with your brand. Like fundraising, Byju revelled in having these conversations with other founders and was constantly looking at acquisition opportunities. During the initial days, he was cautious and keen on acquiring for skills rather than scale. In fact, most of the acquisitions were companies recommended by our investors.

It was during this phase that Pearson, the global education books and content giant, reached out to us with the offer to sell TutorVista—a company they acquired from a serial entrepreneur K. Ganesh of Growth Story few years earlier. The company's sale to BYJU'S at reduced valuation was a sad end to an organization which was once the poster child of Indian edtech during the long-forgotten edtech wave of the 2000s.

India's education sector has always fascinated and lured entrepreneurs. The huge base of 250 million school-going students and 100 million working professionals is one of the

70

largest in the world, if not the largest. For obvious reasons, both money and talent flowed into it to solve the problem of access, affordability and quality in education through technology. However, the sector quickly lost its charm due its complexity and heterogeneity. Entrepreneur after entrepreneur has come in to invest money into the sector seeing early wins (or maybe they felt so), only to invest a lot more and then fail. This ongoing phenomenon has created multiple waves of investments in the sector which I will refer to as the waves in Indian edtech.

The first attempt to revolutionize India's education through technology happened in 1994 and was spearheaded by Shantanu Prakash, an alumnus of IIM-Ahmedabad, who through his firm Educomp started selling smartboards, computers and technology to schools. Over time, he created a smart classroom solution with hardware, software and content. Driven by high-energy selling and easy instalments to pay for the solution (subscriptions), Educomp was able to reach 20,000 schools—an unheard-of feat in the backward Indian school ecosystem. The product comprised hardware, software and content solution which acted as an end-to-end system enabling teachers to train students better. Educomp was able to scale to a Rs 1000 crore-revenue and did a successful IPO in 2006 'showcasing' scaled business in education and technology, only to crash soon when it became apparent that their receivables from schools were not getting collected. Since the focus was a lot on acquiring schools, the company resorted to discounting tactics in a big way to onboard schools. Once onboarded, there was hardly any focus on making the solution a success, i.e., handholding the teachers to use the product and improve the teaching process. Maybe they were confident that their product was so good that teachers would use it on their own. The quality was indeed good, and it could have improved teaching quality by leaps and bounds. Unfortunately, that didn't happen; in fact, the reverse happened. The teachers started seeing the Educomp product as a conspiracy to replace them eventually: a competitor in their classroom. Without the teachers using it, there was no value proposition left and soon schools stopped using the product and discontinued paying the subscription fees, leaving Educomp in the lurch. The company which had taken heavy debts to diversify into new areas in education was soon straddled with all sorts of issues and ended up filing for bankruptcy in 2017. The bad days didn't end there and multiple law suits followed. It was an unfortunate end to a once-celebrated company and something which stained the future of technology in education at schools.[8]

The second wave happened in the early 2000s when TutorVista built a large business centred on Indian teachers tutoring US students. The model made perfect sense—using high-calibre English-speaking teachers of math and science available at economical rates in India to teach the students in the US where such talent is super expensive. The TutorVista platform was able to do acquisition at scale in North America and deliver homework help, lectures and doubt-clearing sessions for school and college students struggling with science, technology, engineering and mathematics (STEM) courses. In the Indian education arena, the company ended up becoming a revered name. The business model, though built on the IT outsourcing fundamentals, was an outcome of looking at outsourcing from

8   Devesh K. Pandey, 'CBI books Educomp Solutions, others in ₹360.30-crore bank fraud', *The Hindu*, 1 May 2022, https://www.thehindu.com/news/national/cbi-books-educomp-solutions-others-in-36030-crore-bank-fraud/article65372964.ece

a very different perspective. In IT services, Indian companies had always picked up low-skill work and moved it to India, while here was a case of outsourcing very high-skill work of training and developing America's next generation. This was the brilliance of the founder, K. Ganesh, and his team, who tried to solve this problem though this opportunity. The company demonstrated scale in education through technology; this time by doing business in the western world and ended up getting acquired by global education giant Pearson for Rs 1000 crore valuation. I was intrigued when Pearson was ready to sell a company for which they had paid a fortune four years ago, to us. Pearson told us that TutorVista was their attempt to do B2C business which didn't go as planned. Under the current leadership, they had decided to focus only on B2B business, their core strength, and were in the process of exiting all B2C businesses. This is a typical reason given by large organizations when they consolidate, but normally, they wait for a fair valuation to materialize for the assets on the block. In this case, Pearson seemed to be in a tearing hurry. Since the acquisition price was attractive, we didn't bother to question their logic and went ahead with the acquisition. Hence, TutorVista and Edurite (a business of worksheets which came along with TutorVista) moved into BYJU'S.

'We never could understand that business and hence got out of it,' one of the Pearson executives involved in the process told me later. 'I get that, but I never understood the tearing hurry till I saw the revenue numbers. The entire thing seems muddled. It's hard to say if the earlier revenue was from the business you sold us or retained,' I responded, not sure if I was sympathizing with them or with us since it was our problem now. 'It's going to be hard to turn it around and if anyone can do it, it is you guys with the B2C capabilities. Entire user acquisition of online was driven by search engine optimization [SEO] and lot of performance burn. Before we acquired the company, they literally used to rank on every possible K-12 topic across STEM courses. You search for any academic question on Google and bang the first result is TutorVista.com. All of it disappeared post a Google search algorithm update, post-acquisition. The entire content library was crawled from other websites and copied into their website. Earlier Google algorithms didn't catch it but now it penalizes such behaviour. So, in no time, we saw the acquisition cost go through the roof and Pearson tolerates no such thing. We tightened the screws and that was the end of hyper growth,' he poured out his frustration.

'You can't really say that there was anything wrong there. If the sites were ranking up earlier and with algo changes ranks disappeared, then it's just the environment change, not copied data. In B2C, you need to anticipate and figure things with these changes. This is daily stuff. Also, the PA [page authority] and DA [domain authority] of those pages would have been high and you should have been able to recover rankings if there was no manual action penalty from Google.' 'What about the repeat customers and referrals? Didn't you guys work on those,' I pushed back. 'This is why we are selling. We don't understand this B2C shit and when you go deep you will know more. I don't want to steal your thunder,' he winked with a smile. The wink was clearly a harbinger of the barrage of bad news I would soon have. However, I felt that if the entrepreneur was still around, such problems would never become this big. They always figure a way out and solve the crisis. That's the entrepreneur's DNA.[9]

9   Ashish K. Mishra, 'The miseducation of Pearson (Byju's TutorVista acquisition explained)', The Ken (India), 19 July 2017, https://the-ken. com/story/byjus-TutorVista-edurite/

TutorVista and then Edurite had indeed built a large business, but it was hard to say from where the growth really came—offline or online. The online business was loss-making till it merged with Pearson's India business. TutorVista must be one of the first companies in education in India which leveraged SEO so well in tutoring and hence had a blue ocean strategy. However, it seemed like a business built to sell; may be because of the founder who was a serial entrepreneur. A serial entrepreneur is a builder. He builds the organization for high growth in a short period of time and then attracts people who can take it forward after him. He is not really someone who wants to nurture it for long; for that he relies on others. Unfortunately, it seemed that people who took over from the entrepreneur weren't able to match his passion or prowess, letting the company slide. When you build a business to sell, you tend to focus on short-term hyper growth without bothering about the long-term sustainability of the business. The assumption is 'Let's get to growth and we will solve for sustainability later', and this works in a lot of cases.

TutorVista had relied on quite a few growth hacks which were ahead of their time, like auto-renewal of subscriptions. Auto-renewal is basically a mechanism where your subscription gets auto-renewed every month and remains active till you cancel it explicitly. This is a common practice in subscription products in the US today. However, TutorVista's homework help and support products were generally used by customers to help them tide over the exam period or a particularly difficult assignment. Customers didn't feel the need to use the product every month and hence the auto-renewal created bad customer experience over time. I sincerely believe that the problem could have been solved if the focus was on cracking what the acquired customers wanted to keep coming back to the platform for.

Today there are hundreds of edtech subscription players worldwide using a similar business model. Added to this the fact that there was not much focus on improving delivery, the company could never build a good repeat and referral channel. After running for almost a year, we also gave up and TutorVista met a similar fate as Educomp. The business was shut down and the second wave also came to a naught.

Both the waves had a lot of elements which were similar. Education companies trying to scale by using technology with disproportionate focus on acquisition and ignoring delivery of education. To open the market, both companies used financing leverage in a big way. There is nothing wrong in it—that's how you open the market and make your product affordable. Ask any BMW salesperson on how they scaled and he will vouch for EMIs. However, when you are allowing the customer to pay while they use, high service standards must be maintained throughout, thereby not allowing the customer to have any second thoughts about continuing to pay for the product. So, this model requires companies to focus disproportionately on delivery, which was never the case. Since that didn't happen, both these businesses ended up making much lower revenues than they anticipated based on their bookings, due to cancellations.

Quick scaling through aggressive sales and marketing, opening up the market through financial leverage—by 2019, these things were true of BYJU'S too. So, I couldn't stop asking myself, 'We are the third wave in India's edtech. Will we also end up like other the two?'

Chapter 11

The Third Wave

At BYJU'S, we managed to build a much larger edtech story than Educomp or TutorVista. The revenue was much bigger and unlike the other two whose cash flows from the beginning were patchy thanks to the subscription model, BYJU'S had solid cash flows. Our company built the business on the back of solid content, aggressive sales and innovative marketing. The collections were always a priority from day one and no products were shipped without realizing the cash in bank after some very early reversals. At least I was determined that we will build a sustainable business and make it 'third time lucky' for Indian edtech.

However, as we continued our growth story, there were trends I found disturbing and which needed immediate action.

First, with field sales and the ability to sell multiple years of content, we ended up realizing the lifetime value (LTV) of the customers with the first purchase itself. In other words, our product and sales team were so good that we were able to sell multiple years of content in one visit. For instance, we normally sold Class VII, VIII, IX and X content to a Class VII student at one go, as against just selling the class VII content.

This was strategically done because field sales as a model was expensive and to make the unit economics work, the average revenue per user (ARPU) needed to be higher. A single-year subscription wouldn't have made the cut. But the unexpected flip side of the extremely successful strategy was the reduction in the importance of retention.

The retention percentage of BYJU'S customers was always high and was in the range of 80 per cent, i.e., of every 100 students who bought a year's curriculum from us, eighty came back next year to buy again. Along with a good product, this was due to the rigorous work of our mentoring team under the leadership of Divya, who tracked the app usage of the students and reached out to them every week to provide the necessary support. They nudged, followed up, handheld and chided, and if nothing else worked, they got the parents involved to ensure the structured curriculum was followed by the student. We had seen a direct correlation between app engagement which is driven by mentors and the outcome the student is able to bring at school and various competitive exams. Mentorship was important to business earlier because it was the chief driver of subscription extension at the end of the year. With multi-year subscriptions becoming the new norm, mentoring grew as a cost centre, with the activity becoming more inbound customer support rather than proactive handholding.

I have always believed that education needs handholding and in most cases, a bit of force and lot of motivation. Given an option, most of us will happily prefer to spend all our time watching movies, reading comics or playing games. Academics only becomes important because of the constant pressure— from parents, peers or society packaged as motivation. The success of an educational product finally is about how gently it can apply that pressure and prod the learner to their personal success. Hence without mentoring, we were becoming a content library and if libraries could educate students, would schools, universities and teachers be needed?

The second and bigger trend related to the sales team. By then, our team had grown into 3300-odd counsellors distributed across sixty-plus offices. These people called customers from the leads we generated, fixed appointment and went to customers' homes to convert leads into sales. By standards of field sales in India, it was a large team but not the largest. Asian Paints had more than 7000 people on the field to manage their dealers, while banks and insurance companies have teams running in tens of thousands. However, the main difference here is that we built this team from scratch in just three years. Our processes were only evolving, and we had been running a very competitive ecosystem. At that scale, I was finding it very hard to control the sales organization which was developing a mind of its own. Though tightly reviewed and managed through an extensive hierarchy, a field sales team was bound to do things which were not as per the standard operating procedure (SOP). The fact that they were on their own with limited scope for automation in processes, combined with the high-pressure environment, ensured that there were always some or the other issues.

To open up the market, alongside instalments, we were also offering a trial period whereby parents could return the product within a limited time period and get a full refund if they were not happy with the product. Since we had great faith in the efficacy of our product, we always encouraged our sales team to leverage this feature while selling and getting the student to start using the product. The product and mentoring were expected to do the remaining work and ensure engagement, thus avoiding the possibility of refund. Since most of the sales

happened with the help of EMIs provided through a finance
partner and the first EMI came into effect post the refund
period, effectively the mechanism allowed the customer (the
student) to experience the full product by just making a down
payment. The pitch was: 'Pay the down payment and try the
product out for 15 days. You can return and get 100% refund
if you don't like it.' I could see all sorts of complaints coming
up since 'retuning the tab' for the refund was not an easy
process. Like any refund or cancellation process followed in the
industry, there were multiple levels of teams involved in trying
to convince the parent and student not to take a refund. The
process at times became tedious and fraught with not-so-good
customer experience due to delays and back and forth. For a
lot of customers who were already unhappy, this was extremely
off-putting. All this along with too much of leeway some of the
leaders provided to sales started creating an environment where
I felt we were losing control of our sales team.

'I don't think we should expand this proprietary sales
channel any more. These people are uncontrollable; I end up
spending two hours every day solving escalations and audit
finds something to blame me as if it's all my fault. From the
perspective of larger strategy and governance, this may be
right, but frankly it's hard to control things to minute levels in
such a super-charged environment.' I cribbed to Byju. 'I want
to expand the sales force. We should make it 10,000 people
and triple our revenue next year. You should hire some good
people who can handle the team. It's no longer your work,' he
responded, clear on his future strategy. 'Sir, I don't understand
why you only think of linear growth by adding people. With
every new guy added, we are seeing a marginal reduction in
productivity. With every step of scaling of leads, we are seeing
the cost increase non-linearly. The revenue is not going to

grow linearly with an increase in counsellors. We have hit the maximum of this channel already. It's time to diversify the channels. We have a great brand now and can easily go deep anywhere in the country. In my view, we should take a two-pronged approach—develop our e-commerce and retail channels for metro/tier 1 cities' customers. For smaller towns, where it is essential to have a representative to sell a product of this ARPU, use a franchisee and channel partners network,' I presented to him the thought process I had been working on. He disagreed. 'You have been running pilots for e-commerce for long with no RoI. Same is our experience with franchisees. These people can't work at our pace. We may be the largest, but we have barely scratched the surface of this 250 million people market.' I responded somewhat impertinently: 'E-commerce will never work when we allow the sales team to give higher discounts. For franchisees, you had the wrong guy running it. You can't create a partner network by constantly competing with them. In the first few years, you should let them grow and make money and, most importantly, we should have patience.' Byju had already made up his mind that our then current model was the right model to educate a billion-plus Indians and he would have nothing of what I presented. Hence, I kept my reservations to myself and started working on stronger processes to prevent these trends from blowing out of proportion.

Even though I was not in alignment with some of his decisions, they did undeniably set new standards, not just in edtech but other industries too that rely on inside sales and field sales. To reach his 10,000-strong sales team, we hired from all possible tier-2 and tier-3 engineering colleges and paid them a starting salary of Rs 7 lakh fixed and incentives. The salary was princely and ended up changing the benchmark for the entire industry. And the most important change was that there was no regional disparity. Someone passing out of Government College of Engineering Kannur and employed in our Kannur office would be offered the same package as someone recruited from R.V. College of Engineering (Bengaluru) and working out of our corporate office. It was nothing short of a revolution in salaries for smaller cities. If today, students coming out of tier-2/3 colleges are getting paid well, large part of credit goes to one man—Byju. His scale and success have spawn many tech entrepreneurs who have tried to follow the same model thus adding to the flywheel of prosperity in tier-2 and tier-3 towns.

Threats in the Horizon

When we were selling our product, one question frequently posed to us was: why pay so much money for videos when one can consume it free on YouTube? We had a clear-cut pitch to tackle that objection. However, it was visible to us that YouTube could spawn a business model which could compete with us due to the sheer distribution might. I saw it as a non-proprietary distribution channel which any new entrepreneur could leverage to create a business. Very similar to our learning app in digital and sales team in offline—our proprietary distribution channel which we built for ourselves. YouTube at scale was much bigger and crowdsourced and hence had much more content. Theoretically, it was free, but practically speaking, the many ads came in the way when trying to learn something. After so many years of working with students, it was clear to us that merely having content on a website, even if it was structured like Khan Academy's, could not deliver an outcome. For the simple reason that learners do not have so much of self-motivation, and it needs someone to bring discipline—a mentor. However, what if the entrepreneur decides to do a freemium model on YouTube like we do with our app. That is, the entrepreneur allows the learners to freely consume the content on the YouTube channel. Once they start loving the content, he invites them to attend paid advanced sessions with him on his website or app. At that time nobody was doing it and everyone was happy getting paid from the ads which showed on their channels and worsened the experience of the learner. I was however sure that someone would do so soon.

While BYJU'S was basking in its glory and refusing to see the future, there were multiple new models emerging in India's edtech horizon. The huge success we achieved both in revenue and valuation was attracting smart entrepreneurs into the sector. Funded by VCs who missed the BYJU'S bandwagon, these new edtechs were opening up the market with new models which were slowly beginning to compete with BYJU'S. At least one thing seemed clear to me: if BYJU'S was the third wave in India's edtech, then we are not alone in this wave. This time, it was a tsunami, and we were one of the players who were propelling the wave—probably the biggest then. Unfortunately, we were turning a blind eye towards the challengers who were not smug like us and were trying to solve the problem of engagement and outcome. Though nobody else in the company felt so, I believed that our leadership of the market was under threat.

Chapter 12

YouTube Education

Gaurav Munjal is a straight talker and a go-getter and he makes it a point to mention that before a meeting. 'I may use language and words during our review meetings that qualify as harsh in the corporate world. But I will also send out a public apology on the company WhatsApp group later if that happens in the heat of the moment,' Gaurav seemed to be bursting with excitement out of his black expensive jacket with an Apple logo on it. I couldn't stop myself from observing his obsession with Apple and Steve Jobs. His office, his classrooms, his apps—everything drew inspiration from the Apple ecosystem. And so did his obsession for making great products and focus on design and quality. Skills essential for an entrepreneur to succeed and scale in the start-up world.

'I still come to office every day and put in ten hours. I'm involved in everything—product, strategy, marketing. Some call it "micromanagement", but that's okay. I need results and I need quality in those results. Most importantly, I need it quickly!' he stated emphatically. 'At least the guy is honest and realizes his strengths and weaknesses,' I thought. 'He is definitely not as bad as the media has painted him to be.' 'How do you manage to respond on WhatsApp so fast?' I asked him.

'I'm very involved in everything, and I track everything through WhatsApp and Slack. All I'm looking at is that kind of involvement from my leaders,' Gaurav beamed. 'Doesn't he get distracted between his review meetings if he is going to respond to every message in a minute?' I thought but decided not to ask the young entrepreneur who seemed to be proud of his turnaround time on WhatsApp.

Gaurav is not alone in his obsession to be on 'top of things on WhatsApp'. I have recently met another entrepreneur—famous for blurring the lines between being an entrepreneur and an investor—not able to hold a ten-minute meeting without checking his WhatsApp screen and responding to messages. These people can sure type fast! I have met a lot of WhatsApp managers in my career—the new breed of young managers who prefer to give the gospels of management on their team WhatsApp group rather than sitting and mentoring the team members individually on their process, data and pitch. I guess when some of them grow up and start their own companies, they end up becoming WhatsApp entrepreneurs.

Gaurav stumbled on the idea of Unacademy in 2010 when he used YouTube to upload a video of himself teaching a computer graphics course. The video was intended for his friends who wanted him to go to their dorm and teach them for the exam next day. But Gaurav changed his plans and decided instead to make a video and send it to his friends through YouTube. Nobody complained. In fact, his friends were happy that they could rewatch the parts they couldn't follow. Thus, the idea of Unacademy was born.

Unacademy was launched as a YouTube channel focused on college students in 2010 while Gaurav was studying for his engineering at NMIMS. Post his BTech, while continuing the

channel as a side gig, Gaurav went to work at Bhavin Turakhia's
Directi as a developer. The entrepreneur in him could hardly
continue as an employee and within a year, he started his
venture Flatchat, a platform that helped college students find
accommodation. Gaurav's go-getter attitude and love for social
media were evident during this period itself. He was one of
the people who routinely responded to the tweets of Rahul
Yadav, the once-high-flying and quickly discredited founder of
Housing.com. To give Gaurav due credit, his responses were
witty, and this grew his followership quickly as an outspoken
and sensible underdog in the same sector compared to the
high-handed Yadav. Gaurav was joined by Hemesh Singh
(co-founder of Unacademy) during his Flatchat days, and
they managed to sell the company to Commonfloor by 2014.
Later, Commonfloor was acquired by Quikr and Flatchat was
shut down. However, the big turning point in Unacademy
came when Gaurav convinced his childhood buddy Roman
Saini to join as Unacademy co-founder. In 2015, Roman,
Hemesh and Gaurav launched Unacademy.

It is said that there are three ways of getting successful:
working very hard, getting lucky or being a born genius.
The third one is true of Roman—a prodigy who cleared the
prestigious AIIMS admissions test at the age of sixteen and
glided through UPSC with rank 18 at the age of twenty-two.
In 2015, the Unacademy channel, with Roman as its face, had
around a million views per month. That was also when they
focused on UPSC prep.

The UPSC Civil Services is undeniably one of the most
prestigious exams in India as its toppers land bureaucratic
posts. Nearly 11 lakh students take the exam every year
and the top 180 students are selected after two rounds of
written exams and a round of interview to become part of

our nation's steel backbone—the Indian Administrative Service. Lower ranks pick up equally prestigious services like the Indian Foreign Service (IFS), Indian Police Service (IPS), Indian Revenue Service (IRS), etc. If one goes by the simple arithmetic of selection as an IAS to the number of applicants, the conversion rate for becoming an IAS is 0.016 per cent. An application to Harvard University has a 3 per cent chance of success and 1.5 per cent of 11 lakh JEE applicants get a seat in the IITs. Hence, the huge denominator, insane popularity of the exam and the limited seats easily make UPSC the world's hardest process to crack. It's ironical that our bureaucracy which is made up of people who come through this filter is still one of the most inefficient in the world. Roman, who became part of the storied group, left IAS in two years and teamed up with his friend to launch Unacademy. I'm sure Roman might not have thought too much of this 0.016 per cent conversion; after all, he had cracked AIIMS which has fifty MBBS seats and a lakh applicant, which is a conversion rate of 0.05 per cent and then left his career as an AIIMS doctor within a year, for UPSC.[10]

Thanks to Roman's profile, and the insights and depth he and his team brought to the Unacademy content, the channel quickly became popular among UPSC aspirants. In an exam

[10] M. Sriram and Chandra R. Srikanth, 'Pure aggression: Inside Gaurav Munjal and Unacademy's quest for growth', 18 March 2022, MoneyControl https://www.moneycontrol.com/news/business/startup/pure-aggression-inside-gaurav-munjal-and-unacademys-quest-for-growth-8211161.html
DNA Web Team, 'Meet Roman Saini, who left his IAS officer job after a year to create a Rs 14,000 crore company', 18 August 2021, https://www.dnaindia.com/business/photo-gallery-meet-roman-saini-who-left-his-ias-officer-job-after-a-year-to-create-a-rs-14000-crore-company-upsc-exam-mbbs-unacademy-gaurav-munjal-hemesh-singh-2906598

where every single question, chapter and input matters, learning
from a UPSC prodigy was a much-coveted USP Unacademy
offered. This helped them get to scale as an add-on learning
resource for the students who were already enrolled and learning
from a Rajendra Nagar coaching centre—the Mecca of UPSC
coaching in Delhi. Roman joining and creating the UPSC
product was truly a milestone in the Unacademy journey.
However, there was another thing Gaurav did early on quite
serendipitously that would help Unacademy in a big way later
in the journey—his decision to launch a YouTube channel.

YouTube as a phenomenon was growing steadily in India
in 2015–16, with more and more people preferring to spend
their time online watching videos rather than reading articles.
However, with the launch of Jio at the end of 2016 and its
revolutionary pricing, access to video on phone became the
default reason for going online. The effect was so pronounced
that Facebook prioritized trying to position themselves as a
video-first social network. However, the biggest beneficiary of
this change was YouTube. It literally became the place everyone
now went to kill time, get entertained, ask a question, get
motivated and learn something new. Suddenly, Unacademy,
with its channels, became a brand exposed to millions of
people who thronged to YouTube to learn about current affairs
required for UPSC, Bank Probationary Officer and other
government exams.

By 2019, Unacademy had 13 million free learners, 10,000
educators and no business model (or revenue). Those were the
days of stupendous growth and investments of BYJU'S and the
joke which ran in the market was that there were three kinds
of edtech investors—those who invested in BYJU'S and made a
killing, those who missed BYJU'S early and were waiting to get
in soon and finally those who missed BYJU'S and were looking

for an alternative in edtech. Gaurav realized this and pitched Unacademy as that alternative. His pitch was simple: 'BYJU'S is a sales and marketing company and grew on the back of their superb execution of both, but after a point, it's not a business that can be scaled nonlinearly. While Unacademy is a product-tech company. Our approach is to solve education through product interventions.' The pitch worked well and was backed by an impressive top of the funnel i.e., more than 13 million free learners who were engaging intensely on the Unacademy channel. The strategy they presented was to monetize the base by building an app where premium offerings would be sold to the same base. The idea worked and they were able to position Unacademy as an alternative to BYJU'S to desperate investors who wanted a win in the world's largest K-12 education ecosystem.

Though Unacademy had been raising money since 2015, valuation started hitting above $100 million from 2018. Both in 2019 and 2020, they were able to double the valuation with the addition of impressive new investors. They even managed to get Sequoia, which was a key investor in BYJU'S, on their capitalization (cap) table. This happened because Gaurav and team were able to demonstrate their vision of top-of-the-funnel increase in traffic and engagement using YouTube and productization of education thesis by launching the Unacademy app. The app offered premium classes from educators who then moved their free audience from YouTube to the app. In some way, he replicated the coaching-centre model where educators are a big part of driving conversions.

With a war chest now, Gaurav and his co-founders attacked the biggest coaching market in India—JEE. If there was one thing Unacademy did exceptionally well at this point, it was the campaign they used for launching their JEE product. Shrewdly, they picked up Kota, India's largest coaching destination—literally a city full of aspiring JEE students. The city is infamous for its unhealthy teaching methods and extreme pressure students have to go through while studying.

Unacademy sponsored a YouTube series called *Kota Factory,* which was about the life of students (preparing for competitive exams) in Kota and how they struggle. The story had very smart product placements and branded content which struck a chord with its TG. Suddenly, Unacademy emerged as an alternative for lakhs of students who were frustrated with Kota. Gaurav followed it up with what he called the Unacademy anthem—a video song, again pushed through YouTube, which celebrated the students' struggle and studying from anywhere on Unacademy. With the help of its seventy-plus channels, Unacademy pushed this content to virality, leveraging the power of YouTube and precisely reaching their TG because by then the TG of edtech, especially ones in test prep, has completely moved to YouTube from TV. They had hit the bull's eye.

YouTube is an interesting partner to a brand's growth and Unacademy was one of the first brands in India to really leverage it. Once they had the audience, they started aggressively selling to them using the great feedback they had received while pushing free content. The model was a success and soon they started generating revenue. However, the best was yet to come, and it was something nobody—not even Gaurav—had ever dreamt about.

Chapter 13

Replacing Classrooms Live

In 2006, Google bought a nascent but upcoming video streaming website called YouTube for $1.65 billion—a princely sum then. Google agreed to pay so much for YouTube because they correctly saw the trend of online customers moving from text and images to videos, and YouTube had a massive share of the video pie on the internet. However, even Google could not have imagined the impact YouTube would have on educating the world. Over the years, a ton of education brands were built on YouTube. Notable among these was Khan Academy, founded by Salman 'Sal' Amin Khan, an MIT-Harvard graduate who was one of the first to leverage the power of videos and YouTube to build a highly visible education brand. A brand that motivated thousands, if not millions, of teachers to do the same. The crop of edtech entrepreneurs from India were no different.

Khan Academy was launched as a YouTube channel when Sal's tutoring of his niece Nadia on a Yahoo! Doodle notepad triggered more such requests from his relatives. He moved to YouTube to implement a one-to-many format from one-to-one. YouTube also allowed him to prevent repeating since now the kids could play and replay the videos based on their learning pace. The videos went viral in the US market where the tutors with an Ivy League profile like Sal were charging nearly $100 per hour for such lessons. The channel had 7.7 million followers in 2022 and is the predecessor of literally everything that has happened in the current phase of edtech which is all about educating through engaging videos. Notably, Professor Andrew Ng, the founder of Coursera and Stanford University authority on artificial intelligence (AI), had stated Khan Academy as a huge inspiration behind the Massive Open Online Courses (MOOCs) revolution which Coursera started. So, we can conclude that YouTube always had a huge role to play in the edtech revolution as the flattening platform that gave access at unprecedented levels.

Sal basically made use of YouTube as a platform for education long before Gaurav did the same at a smaller scale. How did Unacademy become one of the largest-valued education companies in the world while Khan Academy went nowhere business-wise? The answer lies in the banal topic called the business model. Unacademy is probably the first education company globally to have successfully transitioned its free users on their YouTube channel to paid users on the app at such a large scale. This is the reason why it was able to win the pole position in the race for edtech investments. Khan Academy could have monetized it much more easily considering their great reputation, but they decided to take a non-profit route. They were able to get the commitment of funds from the Bill & Melinda Gates Foundation and never really bothered about creating a model which paid for itself. More about this later.

Similar to Khan Academy, there were hundreds of teachers from smaller towns in India who used YouTube effectively to spread their teaching and grow their reputation. All of them saw their YouTube channel providing add-on income to their (offline) tuition earnings or as a way to get more students to their regular classes. The income from YouTube was only through ads. Seen that way, these teachers were more of YouTube influencers with a large following who of course didn't sell products like influencers. They only sold their own teaching services.

Unacademy did it differently. Like BYJU'S, they understood that students need to be actively pushed to learn more and better, and their parents only pay when there are outcomes. For this, unlike BYJU'S, they relied on their existing fanbase on YouTube rather than a paid marketing base—a fundamental difference here from a marketing perspective. While companies like BYJU'S had to spend more and more on platforms like Google and Facebook to bring customers to their app which they then converted, Unacademy focused on their free users on YouTube and converted them. They basically implemented a neat marketing funnel. From an investor's perspective, this was an extremely interesting proposition since all investors were worried about the customer acquisition cost and the dependence on the hegemony of Google-Meta-Microsoft in the world of user acquisition.

Unacademy leveraged their YouTube fanbase to crack free to paid. They further differentiated themselves from BYJU'S by selling live classes rather than video lessons. This was a trend emerging before Covid-19 itself. Thanks to the aggressive BYJU'S engine, students and parents across the country were looking for versions of online learning they were comfortable with. Since it was about replacing the classroom education which they were used to for ages, they tried to rationalize the shift by asking for a version where students could get their doubts solved as and when the class happened, just like in a regular classroom. From this need or bias emerged live online classes. Unacademy recognized this trend early on when they were doing UPSC coaching since UPSC students are hyperactive in classrooms. Without the feature of questioning and learning more, there was no UPSC product.

Though Unacademy was the most visible, they were not alone in the live-class revolution. Multiple new companies in edtech started selling on the premise of attending the class of star teachers live, like a classroom. A company which was able to do it effectively and with scale was Vedantu. Founded by three youngsters who built and sold a successful coaching institute Lakshya, Vedantu was quickly able to establish itself as a leading live learning option in K-12 and test prep. While both Vedantu and Unacademy were able to raise money around the thesis, the big growth happened when a tiny virus shut down all schools and coaching centres in 2020.

The pandemic was a defining opportunity for live players such as Unacademy and Vedantu. An event which gave their products and brand acceptability beyond their wildest expectations. With schools shut, classrooms literally moved online, suddenly Unacademy and Vedantu were the best versions of classes a student could get. This started the mad growth in free users on their platforms and YouTube channels, and all credit to them that they managed to convert a good number of these users into paid customers with good products and clinical execution. With growth in users and revenue came investments at astronomical valuations, thanks to all the cheap money which flowed into the market from the central banks of rich nations. Unacademy's valuation grew from $229 million in 2019 to $3.4 billion in 2021 through four rounds of fundraising during the pandemic.

Vedantu also acquired the coveted unicorn status thanks to the stellar growth they demonstrated during the pandemic.

Covid-19 was an event that changed every sector of edtech by leaps and bounds. However, the exuberance was short lived and as the nation started opening up, students started moving back offline, and online numbers began dipping. That's a story for future chapters.

Chapter 14

The Media Mogul

The conference room looked hazy on screen and Mayank Kumar was seated little farther leaving the chair closer to the screen empty. 'Let's wait a minute for Ronnie,' he said after a brief introduction.

Mayank co-founded upGrad with Ronnie Screwvala and Phalgun Kompalli in 2015 and built it into a formidable company in the promising higher-edtech space. We were waiting for his co-founder-cum-lead investor Ronnie Screwvala, the famous movie maker who post leaving Disney, took an unexpected turn in his career to start an edtech company. He could have chosen the regular K-12 sector considering the scale of his ambitions. Thanks to Mayank and his rich background in higher education, they decided to make upGrad a higher education online company.

The interview was at 3 a.m. PST (Pacific Std Time) and I would have loved to finish it off soon and go back to bed except for my curiosity about why Ronnie and Mayank, two extremely successful people by any standards, decided to get into edtech. 'We believe the working professional segment is where online learning fits best. They need flexibility and are used to learning things online at work,' Mayank explained with Ronnie nodding. 'But isn't the TAM [total addressable market] small when compared to 260 million school-going students?' I asked. 'Now now! Don't start like an investor. This is exactly what an outsider looking at a company from a metric lens will say, but that's not true,' Ronnie intervened and responded in his typically forceful style. 'TAM is not small. There are 80 million-plus taxpayers in India alone. If I just take the LinkedIn base of people earning above Rs 5 lakh a year and students in their final year of colleges, we get a 100 million addressable market.' Just then I realized how little I knew about edtech in India, a field I considered myself an expert in. I heard myself responding to them: 'From a 260 million addressable population, around 10 million can afford a product like BYJU'S, Unacademy or Vedantu, which has a price tag of Rs 25,000. Seen that way, the addressable market of higher ed is much bigger. Add to it, the fact that the stakeholder map is not as complex, the proposition becomes impressive.' Little did I know that in time, I would find more reasons to position higher ed as the next big thing in Indian edtech. That interview marked a new chapter for me—higher edtech and the next phase of my career in an emerging sub-segment of edtech.

Ronnie started his entrepreneurial career manufacturing and selling toothbrushes. The business is still the largest toothbrush manufacturer in the country and manufactures toothbrushes for most of the leading personal care brands. His interest in drama took him to media and he pioneered cable TV in India. He has often told us how hard it was to establish cable TV in India and it was only his indomitable entrepreneurial spirit that kept him going. After selling off the business, he started his media journey launching UTV—a company which redefined media in India. As a kid growing up in the 1990s, his soaps, such as *Shanti* and *Sea Hawks*, with thier fast-paced storytelling and peppy action, were a refreshing departure from the conventional Doordarshan serials. Literally starting from zero, he built his media company into a full stack organization complete with a movie production unit, distribution company, gaming company and animation studio. In this journey, his key supporter and investor was Rupert Murdoch—a monumental figure in global media and founder of Fox–Sky Studios. Murdoch literally found Ronnie and bet on him—a bet which worked really well for Murdoch since UTV was eventually acquired by Disney and Ronnie became the CEO of Disney India. With Disney and Murdoch, Ronnie made some of the most memorable movies of India cinema like *Rang De Basanti*, *Lakshya* and *Swades*.

It came as a surprise to everyone following Ronnie's career when he decided to start an education company after an era in which he was one of the biggest movers and shakers in media. 'I wanted to do something that would deliver quality at scale. I have always done the same in my career and I felt if I can do it with education, then I really would make an impact on the youth of India,' Ronnie told me. The decision to start upGrad, initially known as Ueducation, originated with Ronnie. He partnered with Mayank and brought him as his co-founder. He couldn't have wished for a better partner in this business. As one of the top and upcoming consultants at Parthenon and then Bertelsmann, Mayank already had vast experience and a deep understanding of the education ecosystem, particularly the higher education sector. When given the responsibility to set the strategy of the company,

Mayank identified the potential of the higher education segment and convinced Ronnie to move the company in that direction. He later brought in Phalgun as the third co-founder to handle operations.

For the uninitiated, in 2022, only 29 per cent of Indian students who were eligible to join a university actually joined. The rest dropped out or discontinued their education after schooling. Technically, this ratio (actual enrolment as a proportion of those eligible to join) is called gross enrolment ratio (GER) and is an important metric used to measure a country's progress. For developed nations this percentage is in the high 80s, and for a developing nation like India, ideally the number should be closer to 60 per cent.

Mayank and Phalgun deeply understood this sector, thanks to the multiple projects they had done in this segment, and identified three reasons for the low GER in Indian higher education:

- Access: Most students in India lack access to a good university or college in their home town. The prospect of moving from their home for good education is both unaffordable and a culturally alien concept for them.
- Affordability: Even if there is a college closer to home, for most students it's unaffordable.
- Quality: Colleges which are affordable and not too far from home lack in quality education and thus outcomes. So, students and parents don't feel it's worth spending their hard-earned money on these institutions.

For long, the Government of India tried solving the GER problem through university expansion and proliferation.

The sector, though part of state subject list, has got crores of funding from the central government since Independence. When the combined might of the central and state governments couldn't create enough universities for the youth, the government liberalized university education by allowing deemed universities and private universities and even starting an open university—Indira Gandhi National Open University (IGNOU). An open university is one which provides degrees to students without imposing the condition that students and teachers should be present at the same location during the class hours. Students study part-time and without regular face-to-face classroom interaction and get a degree completed in distance learning mode on passing. None of these measures could really solve the GER problem and the number marginally increased from 24 per cent in 2012 to 29 per cent in 2022.

The founders of upGrad built the organization with the objective to solve this triumvirate of problems. They concluded that it is impossible to build enough universities in India to get the GER to 60 per cent in the immediate future. Hence, their strategy was to solve this problem by building an online platform which will be able to replicate all the tools of learning a high-quality university employs to teach. Thus, upGrad was born.

'In higher ed, we sell formal online university degrees, diplomas and certificates to working professionals. This is a very mature customer we are dealing with and our focus has been to deliver outcomes. We are able to get 87 per cent of our students to complete the course in UGC-prescribed timelines and majority of them get the outcomes they are looking for, i.e., a new job in a new sector, a promotion in their current job or huge professional confidence to do their job better,' Mayank explained to me. 'I don't understand why completion is such a big deal. When they are paying so much, don't they anyway complete the course?' I questioned his stats. 'That's the whole point why we exist. As you have mentioned earlier, education is forced and not something learners will do if they have other options to spend their time on. Take for instance the MOOCs like Coursera and Udemy; they have a completion rate of 2 per cent. While we, with our product interventions and mentors which we learned from you guys in K-12, are able to make 87 per cent of our learners complete their course within the university-defined timelines, i.e., three months to two years depending on which course they are taking. UGC and regulators of countries where these universities are present basically put this condition on the courses regulated by them to bring in discipline.' He continued, 'The easy way to understand this is that MOOCs are a digital equivalent of a library while we are the digital equivalent of a university. If libraries could solve the problem of education, universities would have never existed. But they do and they exist because learners are not self-motivated to learn and they need someone to build and execute a structured curriculum which delivers outcomes for them. This is why universities exist and this is why we exist in this online world.'

This is incredible, I thought. I finally felt I had a perfect use case for online learning which fitted perfectly to the need. In K-12, more so in K-10, however brilliant and engaging one makes the product, the kids often lose interest, especially in today's world where we are competing with the *Marvels and Fortnights* for their time. Soon our learning tab becomes a gaming tab and our engaging videos are forgotten. I honestly believed that this problem could be solved with mentors who rigorously become the kids' learning partners. However, BYJU'S implementation of the same was patchy at scale and this is where our engagement started declining. With working professionals, this problem doesn't exist to a large extent. Professionals who come from companies of all sizes are at a certain level of maturity which brings in high levels of motivation to the online course they sign up for. They also typically sign up when they want outcomes such as job change or professional confidence. They pay their hard-earned money for their courses, unlike their fathers' money in the case of K-12 students. Half of the motivation problem gets solved due to this. The rest is done by the product and mentoring team which does it exactly how we had envisaged it in BYJU'S. They track and nudge the learner to follow the structured curriculum—submit assignments in time, attend all classes, respond to quizzes, etc. and thus drive engagement which leads to outcome. The perfect place where online works is the working professional because the user is self-motivated to learn and needs the flexibility of online to fit learning in his or her busy schedule.

Leaving BYJU'S was hard due to two reasons—leaving something you built over years at a juncture when it was at its peak sounded stupid. The second reason was hardest—leaving Byju (my teacher–mentor who became my boss) who trusted me and gave a boost to my career. However, after more than a decade at BYJU'S, part time and full time, it was time for me to try out something new and shift gears to higher education, a new segment of edtech. K-12 though incredibly popular and big by then had obvious gaps in implementation. Maybe it needed competition from other segments to drive innovation just like it takes the luxury automobile segment to invest and create new features which then makes their way to the mass car segment. I considered upGrad an exciting opportunity to complete my 'professional' tryst with education; an opportunity to go and implement what I knew from the K-12 edtech market creation, to a new segment. I had no idea how much this decision was going to change the narrative of edtech in our country and about the tailwinds which would propel me ahead.

Chapter 15

India's Tryst with Higher Education

Mayank emerged into the room where Ronnie and I were sitting and announced with a smile: 'The government finally announced the NEP [National Education Policy] in the budget; Indian universities, top ranked in NIRF [National Institutional Ranking Framework], can give online degrees now. Guidelines of NEP for universities are quite similar to so many things we have been doing for years now.' It was February 2020, and I was in Mumbai visiting the upGrad team. The timing couldn't have been more appropriate—the annual Indian government budget was presented that day and a huge step towards liberalizing higher education had just got announced. This looked like a good omen.

In the ancient times, India had an education system built on the Vedas and dharma. Thanks to the caste system and gender bias, the percentage of our population that had access to this system was limited. When the British became our political masters, they introduced modern scientific higher education and used it as a tool to exercise control over Indians through cultural colonization. In the process of furthering their cause, the British destroyed the traditional system which existed in India for centuries. The merits of this replacement are debatable considering there were no pariahs in this new system and every segment of the society was allowed to acquire higher education. The British India government set up the first Indian universities in Bombay (Mumbai), Calcutta (Kolkata) and Madras (Chennai) in 1857, modelled around universities in London. English and humanities were taught in these universities. Subsequently, the cause of education was taken up by multiple institutions—from missionaries to the Arya Samaj and a battery of reformers.

In 1947, less than 0.1 per cent of our population was enrolled in twenty universities across the country. According to the 2011 census, i.e., after sixty-four years of educational reforms, 8.5 per cent of Indians above the age of fifteen were graduates—a ninety times increase in sixty-four years which translates to a 7.2 per cent compound annual growth rate. This slow growth was due to the approach taken post-Independence—the focus in the initial years was on building high-quality world-class institutions, albeit only a few ones. The founding fathers of our republic continued with the educational reforms, investing in modern scientific education over the Vedic one. Interestingly, they created invisible barriers for entry to these institutions which were controlled more by exposure to information and 'ways of the world' than someone's caste or gender. These institutions—IIMs, IITs, IISc, various central and state universities, and colleges like St. Stephen's and St. Xavier's—were (and still are) some of the finest in the world, but the limited number of seats ensured that only students and parents who knew about these for years and were prepared to ace the admissions process, mostly through dedicated coaching, made it to these institutions.

This gap between supply and demand was not intentional. A university or even a college requires crores of rupees in capital investment. The Kothari Commission, one of the several education commissions which deliberated India's higher education, had proposed allocating 6 per cent of the country's budget to education. This has remained a distant dream and neither the Centre nor any state has been able to breach the 4 per cent mark with regard to budget allocation for education. The regulations also created barriers for quick expansion of the university system. The University Grants Commission (UGC), the apex statutory body created in 1953 for promoting higher education in India, also acts as higher education regulator and puts forth requirements that need to be fulfilled to establish and run universities. The UGC dictates a precondition of 40–60 acres of land and a combined built-up area of more than 25,000 sq. ft towards various facilities for establishing a university. You either need the state or someone with legendary wealth to create a university. Lately, the regulator and the government have woken up to these luxurious requirements and taken action to make the conditions less stringent. As a first step, the UGC has reduced the land requirement for establishing an open university to 5 acres in 2022.[11]

The Indian government realized that its policy of keeping university education a hegemony of the state has not helped the expansion of the country's graduate base. It began to selectively allow private participation in higher education from the late 1980s. Through the 1980s and 1990s, it permitted the establishment of deemed universities, i.e., higher education institutions that can act like a university. As a university, these

---

[11] PTI, 'Land requirements for Open Universities reduced from 40-60 acres to 5 acres: UGC', ThePrint, 20 May 2022, https://theprint.in/india/land-requirements-for-open-universities-reduced-from-40-60-acres-to-5-acres-ugc/964321/

institutions had degree-granting powers and controlled three important parts of the education process:

Entry: Admission process as in test, interview or metrics, based on which a student can be enrolled into the university

Curriculum: Syllabus and methods of education delivery

Exit: Process of assessment, tests and exams, based on which student's proficiency is tested and becomes the basis for granting the degree

The institutions granted deemed-university status were the ones which had acquired legendary status in their own focus area of education. Manipal, SRM and Jamia Hamdard are some of the notable ones which received deemed status and went about building huge student strength.

Distance Learning

The government rightly identified that one of the constraints impacting expansion of higher education is the huge investment required in building a university and tried to solve the same through open distance learning (ODL). ODL is a form of part-time education wherein the learner can study for a degree while working. The format doesn't require a learner going into a physical institution and they are free to learn things at home and just go to write the exam at an exam centre approved by the university. This especially should have helped Indians from backward areas where there existed no educational institution in the neighbourhood. Government launched ODL by establishing IGNOU to grant ODL degrees. Buoyed by the success of IGNOU which produced graduates in thousands from the word go, the government opened up ODL to other large universities—notably Manipal and Annamalai University.

With its huge network of partners and good marketing skills, Manipal, through Sikkim Manipal University (established as a state university in Sikkim), scaled quickly and soon had nearly a lakh students studying towards degrees with them in the ODL mode. The main reason for the huge growth was the awareness created by their network of partners called franchisees who tapped into the inherent demand for higher education in every nook and corner of the country. Other big universities with ODL rights followed suit, like Panjab University, Kurukshetra University, etc., successfully tapping into the franchisee network built by Manipal. In a lot of cases, it was the same franchisee selling ODL degrees of multiple universities. These educational entrepreneurs who were physically closer to the students soon started offering support on behalf of the universities. They did this by establishing what then became famous as learning centres—a temporary teaching and learning infrastructure at their premises where students could come and learn from the teachers and each other. For a country like India struggling with the propagation of higher education, this jugaad model offered an interesting way to quickly grow.

However, in creating franchisees and learning centres, these universities came under the radar of UGC for violation of two covenants in the UGC ODL guidelines: 1. Franchising of education and 2. Territorial jurisdiction.

Education delivery is a process which only a university can handle and with teaching and exams happening in franchisee learning centres, universities in effect allowed franchisees to handle the delivery. Secondly, the UGC clearly demarcates the territorial jurisdiction of a state university as the state where it is established. This is the area from which a university can take admissions for its courses. By taking admissions from across the country for ODL, universities breached this covenant. Though these were the points UGC admonished the universities for, the regulator only did the same after multiple acts of reckless misinformation by franchisees, some of whom started seeing ODL degrees as a huge money-making business. Large-scale marketing campaigns began appearing with wrong information which ended up testing the patience of the regulator.

The cracking of the whip by the regulator along with the reckless way in which certain universities went about admitting students and executing delivery tarnished the image of ODL degrees in India, and both students and employers started seeing ODL degree holders as second-grade talent who couldn't manage to go to a proper university. This pretty much was the death knell of a system which could have changed our higher education landscape. Even today, there are multiple universities and their franchisees which openly breach ODL norms, devaluing the value of an ODL degree with every such act.

Deemed-to-Be University

In the 2000s, India continued its push for more universities by allowing private capital in the university system. A large number of institutions were given deemed-university and deemed-to-be-university status along with tripling the number of IITs and IIMs, thus making quality higher education more accessible to the student population. India also began allowing private universities, creating large advertised names in Indian education of the day like Amity University, Lovely Professional University, Chandigarh University, Vellore Institute of Technology, etc. It is fascinating to see how big these institutions were able to become in a short period and thus further the cause of more graduates. In the process, they also built large businesses which is the fascinating part because education cannot be profit making in India. An educational institution cannot book profits and is supposed to reinvest all the money earned back into education. This is one reason why government was never keen on allowing enterprises to get into this business. However, the beauty of successful businesses is the creative ways in which they are able to make money. So, they kept the learning part non-profit and made money through ancillary services—housing, placements, supplementary learning products, etc. They did all this while maintaining the outcome and quality at scale. Today, the corporate brands recruiting from Amity, VIT and Manipal are the very brands which earlier used to only go to the IITs and IIMs and is a testimony to the success of this model.

By 2022, from a mere twenty (in the late 1940s), the number of universities in India crossed 1000. UGC now lists fifty-four central universities, 459 state universities, 127 deemed universities, twenty-three IITs, thirty-one NITs, nineteen IIMs, twenty-five IIITs, fifteen AIIMS and twenty-two NLUs alongside 470 private universities. However, these 1000 are also not enough for our burgeoning population. In 1947, we were a nation of 250 million people. Now we are a burgeoning 1.4 billion. Our GER, i.e., the number of eligible learners who go to universities and colleges post completion of school, is still only 29 per cent. For a growing nation just starting to enjoy the demographic dividend (a phase in a nation's life when the number of people who can contribute to nation-building is the highest due to the prominence of young in the population), its GER should be in the range of 60–65 per cent. We are still well behind when compared to developed nations or even our competitive neighbour China.

To bridge this GER gap, we will have to literally double our university ecosystem in a short time period. Considering the investment required to set up universities, this task seems an impossibility. The solution? Our New Education Policy, or NEP.

Higher Education

In a nutshell, NEP is applying technology and liberating regulations in education to bring in flexibility and quality. It brings back the concept of degrees in part-time mode, this time through online mode and allows universities to collaborate with edtech firms and deliver degrees online. In the process, it removes the idea of territorial jurisdiction of universities offering online degrees and brings in frameworks on how delivery should be made. Theoretically, this means the top few universities can teach all the students willing to take their degrees online. In practice, the situation has been quite different with most of the big ones not giving degrees online in the name of dilution of quality. NEP however is planning to be ambitious with ideas like Professor of Practice—a part-time role in UGC-approved universities where an expert from industry without a PhD can play the role of a professor—or Academic Bank of Credits (ABC), an unbundling mechanism of credits wherein learners can take credits in a self-paced mode by learning individual courses online and then use the bank of credits accrued to later complete a degree at a participating university. These are revolutionary ideas which can propel our higher education sector into the league of extraordinary. However, how well these will be executed is anyone's guess.

'NEP is a revolutionary document and pretty much covers every idea which is in practice in developed nations, and we adopted in our courses—credit transfer across courses and universities, laddering of certificates, diplomas and degrees based on the years of learning etc.,' Mayank continued. 'It will formalize all these now in India, and at some point, we will be able to start marketing these cool features.' The excitement in the room was palpable. Unlike BYJU'S which operated in K-12 supplementary learning programmes, upGrad sold formal higher education products, i.e., their programmes were degrees which were recognized as graduate and postgraduate school-leaving certificates world over by academia and corporate.

'It will take some time for this to get implemented. So, let's not rush into anything like that. The last thing we want to do is to rub the regulators the wrong way,' Ronnie said and turned to me. 'This sector is very different from what you have been dealing with so far. You will soon understand the nuances. But a big one is that our courses start once in a quarter and can't begin anytime like BYJU'S.' He was talking about the structured batches mechanism followed in higher ed. Being a formal education platform, courses need to start as batches and get completed in a prerequisite duration to qualify for the degree.

Upskilling by taking a course or lifelong learning by going back to academics has never been part of our culture. We believe in learning on the job and are quite good at it. So good that our university curriculum teaches us things which were relevant in the 1970s and still we manage to ace our jobs within days of joining. Growing up in a country which always had a dearth of jobs, a job is the reason why we put effort to educate ourselves. A job is always seen as the 'be all and end all' of life.

The trend began changing with the first generation of IT professionals who after Y2K were forced to upskill themselves in newer technologies to hold on to their well-paid jobs. With the growth of technology-driven jobs upskilling soon became a necessity. Initially, the companies these professionals worked in used to arrange for the upskilling in-house. Soon, techies realized that this upskilling is what will give them quick growth in salaries in their career through job switches and started paying for it themselves.

Higher education platforms like upGrad, Great Learning, Simplilearn and Eruditus were built primarily for these techie working professionals. While Simplilearn focused on short certificate courses, Eruditus followed an online program management (OPM) model. OPM is a model in which the company ties up with a university and takes it courses online, providing a tech platform along with acquiring admissions for the course. Great Learning was started as the online arm of the Great Lakes Institute of Management and soon metamorphosed into an independent online learning company. Both Great Learning and upGrad's offerings were similar in 2020, with both trying to control every aspect of education, from customer acquisition to delivery of content to career services for a techie customer.

Globally, the model for higher education online developed with MOOCs. MOOCs (or Massive Open Online Courses) was created by Dr Andrew Ng, an AI researcher from Stanford, when he launched Coursera. MOOC is basically an online learning platform with videos, live sessions, quizzes and millions of courses of all possible genre and length. Coursera relied on individuals, academic institutions and corporates to create these courses and the success of the platform spawned more players globally. Today, the leading MOOC platforms are Coursera and Udemy, which rely on a business model wherein thousands of courses are given for free in the asynchronous mode and customers are required to pay only if they want a certificate for the course they have finished. The certificate can come from the MOOC, a corporate entity like Google or an educational institution running that course.

This model relies on the assumption that users will come to the platform to acquire knowledge and will be self-motivated in completing the curriculum. Since they have put in so much of effort, they will be keen to get the stamp of certification for their work. Unfortunately, this didn't pan out as expected, and completion rates were poor. Hence these platforms created a B2B or enterprise business model wherein they gave different kinds of access to enterprises for a monthly subscription rate. Using these Coursera and Udemy subscriptions, corporates provide logins to their employees who could now access all the courses in Coursera and get certified as per their upskilling requirement. The enterprise business model was able to help these companies scale and interestingly in India, a large part of their customer base is universities. That is, universities in India are giving digital content to their students with the help of these MOOC platforms.

At the university level, the idea was adopted to create OPMs which focused on formal university certificates and degrees delivered online. In the West, universities have relied on partners to sell their continuing education and part-time courses for long. Over time, some of these partners evolved into OPM companies which along with helping with admissions and services also gave the universities a platform to take their courses, majorly formal degrees, online. US is the largest playground for OPMs and there are a few big ones like 2U and Academic Partnerships that rule the market. The market has been going through a bit of a turmoil and a big OPM Zovio filed for bankruptcy in 2022.

Back in India, due to our cultural obsession with degrees and the way corporates give preference to college degrees over online certificates, the OPM model had a better product market fit. Hence, this is the model key players like upGrad and Great Learning adopted but with one significant difference. Indian customers and universities which they worked with were very different from their Western counterparts. Hence, a light-touch approach where one creates content and leaves it to learners to learn, would never work here. They hence evolved an approach where delivery was more or less handled by these organizations thus ensuring rigour and flexibility. While co-developing content and instructional framework with the universities, they added a service layer to the delivery which ensured outcomes. There were two key aspects to this service layer:

Mentoring/Buddy: Every student gets a mentor or a success manager who closely tracks the performance of the learner on the platform and ensures the learner never falls behind. They reach out and help when a learner misses a submission or bunks a class. In a way, the buddy adds the discipline essential in education.

Career services: The outcomes desired by learners are all connected to a better package. The package often doesn't come just by getting a degree or learning a tech course. Often this transition requires an overall improvement of the learner's personality especially in the areas of soft skills and presentation. This is the work done by the career services team. They literally reboot the learner and make him presentable.

The Indian OPM approach hence has been a full-suite one and literally these companies handle the customer from admission query to job placement. However, the services offered to the university vary depending on the regulatory framework that the university needs to fit into. In India, UGC requires delivery to be done by universities and hence edtechs only provide the platform and add-on services. However, this has changed with NEP 2020 and Indian universities will be open to full-suite engagement soon.

In other words, I was entering the world of higher education just when it was getting liberalized—2020 for university education was almost akin to 1991 for trade.

Chapter 16

Skills of the Future

Growing up, we were always told about the importance of being good at math and English—your tools to a successful career eventually. My mother made sure that I went to the 'best' English-medium school in town and got the best education possible. In a way, she was ensuring that her son was equipped with the skills of the future. While we were busy learning math and English, kids in the West were getting uninterested in those subjects, thus losing their edge in the skills of the future. Our proficiency in these skills, known collectively as STEM (science, technology, engineering and math), which were futuristic during our time, was one of the key reasons why people of Indian origin today occupy key positions in the tech industry. So, we can thank our parents' foresight for our present glory.

'In today's world, built on technology and communication, the skills that will make one successful in future can be very different from what we consider important today. Schools and outdated curriculum are not equipped to get your kids ready for the future.' This was the pitch used by a new breed of edtech start-ups in early 2019 which tried to build a business in the extracurricular/cocurricular space. These organizations predominantly focused on coding as an essential skill kids should have in the new-age world to be successful. The first one to work on this thesis was a company called Camp K-12, but the segment caught the attention of everyone when WhiteHat Jr entered the arena.

The segment of extracurricular skills gained some traction in the metros pre-Covid-19. While the segment had multiple courses like public speaking, writing, advanced math, music, etc., which were delivered online, it was coding which grew fast thanks to the big investment in advertising. WhiteHat Jr and coding business do help us understand how this segment of edtech evolved. However, the story is incomplete without telling the story of the founder who took it to scale—Karan Bajaj.

Karan became a start-up icon because he had an unconventional profile for a businessman. People who knew him will tell you how Karan's success is a testimony to his unbelievable speed and relentless execution; exactly the traits an entrepreneur should possess.

Post his MBA from IIMB, he worked in Procter & Gamble (P&G) Marketing for a few years and would have done well because P&G sent him to the US in a marketing role. This is super rare because a marketer needs to have a cultural understanding of the market he is selling to and getting a marketing opportunity in the US for an Indian kid is very hard. Most of his career was in FMCG marketing across P&G and Kraft Foods, punctured by a short stint in BCG Consulting. His big break came in 2016 when he was appointed as the country head of Discovery India. It is hard to imagine how a person with no media experience and hardly any Indian business experience was given the top role by a prestigious organization. It's one of those enigmas of life which only an ace storyteller like Karan Bajaj can pull off. He must have been masterful.

Karan came to India with the audacious objective of making Discovery big in India. To achieve the same, he embarked on multiple experiments in the name of TAM expansion. Discovery JEET was the most ambitious of all wherein he tried to create a Hindi GEC (General Entertainment Channel) for Discovery with daily soaps. No prizes for guessing what happened. Launched in 2018, it folded up by 2020, by which time Karan had left. Someone who worked with him closely then vouched that he tried his best by pouring his high energy into every aspect of the channel along with millions in investment which burned away in a year. By 2019, Discovery ditched the effort, killed the soaps and started the process of rebranding the channel back as Investigation Discovery. The DSports experiment, launching a sports channel famous for horse racing in India's crowded Sports channel market, also met with a similar fate. In my view, Karan rightly identified that for a sports channel to become big in India, it needs cricket but to fight with the duopoly of Star and Sony on cricket was a long and expensive battle and I don't think Discovery was ready for that. By 2019, Karan had left Discovery to become an entrepreneur and the large hiring he had done for his experiments were getting trimmed. Even today, people who worked with him and were impacted remember him fondly as the guy who tried to help them find a new job in testing times. The stories of Karan writing personal emails to media honchos to help people find a new job is something you will keep hearing from his old staff. He always made it a point to maintain a great relationship with his employees and network, a key skill which helped him go places.

A man of high energy, it's not hard to imagine how well Karan would have done as an individual contributor. A unique aspect about Karan's career is how he takes a sabbatical between roles to write books. At times, the sabbatical is a year-long. He takes an interest in travel, trekking and yoga too. He has written four books, each after a job stint. Of the books Karan has written, two have done quite well commercially while the one he tried to publish in the US received a lukewarm response. The first thing you will notice when you meet him is his discipline and pre-planning. Only someone with an insane degree of discipline and focus can live the way he does. He follows a super-controlled diet and can survive on very little sleep as per people who know him. He always manages to stay at his high-energy levels which he attributes to his daily practise of yoga. There are stories of midnight meetings which ran till 2 a.m. that you can hear from his WhiteHat staff who struggled to keep up with his pace. Interestingly, these stories are narrated proudly, and people remember the times fondly.

WhiteHat Jr was founded as a product company to teach kids coding globally with a structured curriculum delivered by Indian teachers. The idea was powerful and seemed like an excellent opportunity—teaching Western kids coding through Indian teachers. High-quality execution at low cost—a thesis which TutorVista tried to do many years ago. To hit the market quickly, Karan didn't bother to develop his own platform unlike what a Camp K-12 did and used code.org—an open-source coding platform for kids—to deliver his service. He then used the same playbook he used to scale up Discovery JEET—high energy, quick scaling by hiring functional experts and sustained marketing to acquire customers.

In setting up an organization called WhiteHat Jr, Karan displayed unbelievable agility. While creating the sales organization, he would have spoken to literally every big name in the edtech industry. In spite of the fact that field sales was a rage when he was building WhiteHat Jr, Karan followed an inside sales model. This is his depth of thinking since he correctly realized that his TG would predominantly be the urban rich who may not be comfortable with home visits. He evolved a selling model where the teacher did a scripted demo class—a combination of BYJU'S demo and what coaching centres do—as the conversion mechanism. Though the company was built and scaled in months, Karan did multiple experiments and pivots to land at the successful product and business model. So, the speed at which the company grew was a testimony to Karan's speed and his ability to build a team really fast. When you scale that fast, you push your employees to learn at a pace which they may not be capable of and this is where it starts breaking. Till the time the entrepreneur is involved, things work fine since he knows every aspect of the system, its weak points and people. Take the entrepreneur out of the system and it collapses in no time since the people never worked as part of a process; they were simply following a person.

Coding if seen from a TAM perspective was tiny, but Karan and WhiteHat Jr showed that it's possible to create TAM at a blitzkrieg pace. So, it will be wrong to say that Karan knew the company would saturate soon, like a lot of people from WhiteHat Jr team will claim today. The second reason to back this thesis is the fact that Camp K-12 had also met with a similar fate of slowdown, and players like Cuemath and Vedantu, who started coding then, had since shut down the vertical. More than saturation of the market, I see it as saturation of ideas with regards to the new direction the organization can take.

Multiple people in the industry today will claim that the founder had a clear-cut plan to sell the company to a bigger organization from day one, and every function of the organization—product, sales, marketing, customer care, etc.—was built with a short-term perspective of selling soon and exiting. The exit eventually came with BYJU'S buying the company; here again there are multiple experts who claim that it was overpaid for. It is debatable if this is actually true because nobody can be sure about the nature of the deal that will come your way when you sell. The buyer can ask you to stay back and move out only after the company's growth story is demonstrated as repeatable and sustainable. So, these claims are unsubstantiated. However, it is true that Karan was able to scale the company to a monthly booking of Rs 50 crore-plus, and multiple investors confirm that all the money the company raised in around six months was intact in its bank account. This means the company was generating cash for funding its own operations and there was no burn. For such an organization, I don't think Byju overpaid, and it was an astute buy.

Anyway, Karan always seemed to be in a hurry and used the same Discovery playbook to scale. To begin with, the coding product had good reviews and initial customers appreciated how the graphical user interface (GUI)-based coding platform helped their kids create an app quickly. The gratification of building something tangible motivated the kid to sustain the course. This trick not only built engagement in initial days but also generated instant self-gratification which led to garnering good reviews and referrals. It is possible that WhiteHat Jr would have met the same fate as Discovery JEET and stopped scaling since it was a new market and the success of WhiteHat Jr attracted more players like Cuemath, Camp K-12 and Vedantu crowding the nascent market. But before the obstacles to scaling, we can't forget the single-most important reason which triggered a super scaling—Covid-19.

Chapter 17

Covid-19 Stage 1:
Fear as the World Locks Down

Right from December 2019, we began hearing rumours of an unknown respiratory disease creating disruptions in Chinese factories thereby potentially impacting our holiday production and sales in the US. Thankfully nothing like that happened and so when I returned to the US in February 2020 to wrap up things and hand over the business functions, I ignored the warnings going around about a lockdown. It was unthinkable! A country locking down! That didn't even happen during the world wars.

Things started going south in February, with countries going into lockdowns and India banning entry of people from nations with a high Covid-19 count. Along with my family, one person who regularly emailed me asking to come back was Ronnie. I was flattered at the attention heaped on me and felt a lot more excited about the company I was going to join. Succumbing to all that good advice, I found a direct flight to India since countries which generally were pitstops on the way from the US to India—Germany, France, the UAE— were all getting into the no-travel list for Indians.

The crowds of masked people was a new sight at the airports and in planes then, and in March 2020, it was a scary sight which reminded of the scenes of *Resident Evil*. Are we all going to die? On the flight back home, I started rationalizing to myself: 'We Indians have exceptional immunity; after all, we have lived and grown up in some of the most polluted and disease-prone surroundings. I'm sure our immunity built against super viruses will take care of this piddly virus even if it manages to attack India.'

The first person I spoke to after reaching home was Mayank, who told me how with so much of uncertainty going around, working professionals were delaying the purchase of upGrad products and revenue which was ahead had fallen behind the plan. 'Our country is very vast and complex for something like this to impact decisions so soon. I suspect it's the sales team who found an easy reason now,' I replied and continued. 'However, from what I have seen all the way through my journey, this is potentially going south. So, consumer sentiments can nosedive quite badly. Hence, we should first focus on collections. Just ensure whatever sale has been booked is collected. Typically, the finance companies are the ones who get risk-averse first and they will stop approving customer EMIs. So, before that happens, please ask the teams to clear the collections. Ideally, activate the credit card EMI option as a back-up.' Mayank agreed with my assessment. I had seen this happen twice in the last few years—first during demonetization and second immediately after the IL&FS (a leading finance institution in India which went bust) crash. The fear of money being sucked out of the market scares non-bank financial companies (NBFCs) and banks which then reduce loan disbursals, making approvals stricter. We spoke about the burning issue every company of the day was trying to decide on—should we shut down office and allow people to work from home? 'We don't have any reported case yet in the office, but people are scared to come out of home,' Mayank explained his conundrum. 'With so much of news going around, keeping the office open is only leading to more worry. upGrad anyway has the ecosystem to work remotely—employees have laptops, our data and tools are on cloud, the product is completely online, video production can happen remotely, and most importantly, there is limited field sales which I can pivot to inside sales quickly. In my view, we should announce remote working immediately, keeping employees' well-being in mind and bring absolute clarity at every level that we need to make it work. That will put an end to these rumours and complaints and productivity will go up.' I found it amusing that all my views of how it is impossible to work from home changed with my short stint in the US. There, I saw how people were comfortable working from anywhere—sharing code on GitHub, taking reviews on Zoom and tracking performance on Tableau. It was more of a response to management needs which evolved post-globalization that created teams for them to manage in India, China and South America. After working in that mode for a year and creating a team in India to leverage the skill arbitrage on capabilities like digital marketing and web development, I could see how a company like upGrad could quickly pivot to a 100 per cent online company—thanks to the foresightedness of the founders who built the infrastructure years ago.

Next day, upGrad became one of the first organizations in India to announce remote working. While many others were still debating whether to announce remote working or not, Prime Minister Narendra Modi decided to speak to the nation on 25 March 2020. People anticipated what was coming—the Sensex tanked and Indians embraced the eventuality. Something which was unthinkable for me just days ago happened and the nation locked down on the 25 March 2020, six days before I changed my job and took over the leadership of upGrad.

The Covid-19-induced lockdown presented unprecedented challenges to the industry as a whole. What it threw up was something none of the established companies had ever experienced, thus giving the start-ups which relied on a first-principles-approach advantage.

The immediate response to Covid-19 across companies, customers and employees was panic. Nobody, how much ever experienced he was, had ever faced a lockdown in their career and hence had no idea how to tackle it. Corporates were worried about money since business got severely impacted affecting cash flows. There was no clarity as to when the business and cash flows would resume. How do we pay salaries without cash? Employees were panicking since they knew companies would have to cut costs and hence the axe could fall on them. Would they have their jobs? Customers were not sure if they would have their source of income and hence suddenly stopped spending on non-essentials. They cocooned up in their homes and started planning their finances to extend the lifeline in case of adversity.

For me, it was an interesting situation. For any organization, the easiest way to cut cost is to reduce marketing, stop hiring and revoke job offers. This is much less painful than terminating experienced employees and shutting down projects. So, I did not rule out the possibility of upGrad revoking its offer to me. However, nothing like that happened and they remained steadfast behind me and the new strategy we were building for upGrad.

I joined upGrad as CEO-India on 1 April 2020 and started meeting my team remotely. The experience was new for most people in upGrad and I was amazed at the speed with which they adapted during a crisis. Necessity is truly the mother of adaptation! The first meeting with the entire organization was a townhall scheduled on the morning of the day I joined. Ronnie and Mayank had told me that the organization was taking some tough decisions to conserve cash and we were going to communicate the same to our employees at the 1 April townhall. Till then, all townhalls in upGrad were led by Ronnie, the master orator. A stickler for time, Ronnie would join three minutes early and take count of the number of employees who joined on time. On Zoom, he could finally get the precise number joining on time and made sure everyone knew that.

Ronnie started by explaining the unprecedented situation we were all facing but reassured everyone that upGrad wouldn't resort to any knee-jerk reaction, like retrenching manpower. He requested everyone to be productive remotely, without being in the line of sight of their managers and help our learners with all support. 'This is when they need our help the most. Help them with the right courses which will make them ready for the future. That's exactly what we have always done. Train them in the skills of the future,' he asserted. 'I have two announcements to make today—one, we have a new CEO, Arjun, who will now share the work of running the organization with Mayank. Please join me in welcoming him to upGrad and wishing him all the best. Second, we will all have to take cuts in our salaries to tide through these difficult times. HR will individually reach out to each of you and communicate the details.' Ronnie closed his speech with that remark to pin-drop silence. 'What a great way to get introduced,' I thought. 'At least he announced my joining upGrad before the pay cut. So, people would have heard about me,' I reassured myself.

What happened at upGrad was a minor response to the Covid-19 pains—thanks to Ronnie who didn't get spooked by the pandemic. Other companies reacted violently, with large-scale firing ravaging across the industry.

The response to Covid-19 by various corporate honchos directly depended on how much money they had in the bank and how soon it would run out. While the bigger corporates focused on employee health and ring-fencing them against risks, the smaller enterprises were looking at a shutdown since they couldn't even keep the business running without opening offices. An optimist like Byju saw that schools and coaching centres were closing down making his app ubiquitous and saw his huge growth in traffic as the prequel to the arrival of edtech as a dominant force in education. Gaurav Munjal was excited that his Kota-targeting campaign was finally working since Unacademy had emerged as an alternative for students in Kota after the city was forced to shut down. Higher education companies like Great Learning and Simplilearn which had not taken investment decided on a wait-and-watch approach and restricted investment and people. Extracurricular learning-firm WhiteHat Jr doubled down on pushing their product as a great option to keep the kid sitting at home engaged while acquiring a new skill. It ended up being a great solution to parents working from home and struggling to engage their kids meanwhile. Then on, how we all responded to this adversity pretty much defined us.

Chapter 18

Covid-19 Stage 2:
Resurgence and Finding Your Feet

When in doubt, ask the person who will never lie to you—the customer. This is something I have always followed in my life. So, when faced with the uncertain times of the initial Covid-19 days, I went back to my customer—this time the working professional. I listened to hundreds of calls and heard what the customer was telling the counsellor—their aspirations, dreams, fears. I spoke to our counsellors to validate my thoughts and looked at data over years to understand the patterns. After days of research alongside the daily grind of trying to establish myself at upGrad, I went to the founders with my hypothesis.

'I want to go aggressive, marketing our courses. I have been listening to the customer voice and I can clearly see the uncertainty and denial making way to acceptance and what-next, albeit slowly. Though there is a lot of uncertainty, our customers today have the time to take our courses alongside their jobs, a very strong need to upskill since technologies are changing at fast clip thanks to remote working, and most importantly, discretionary income since they are not spending on their rent, travel or entertainment. There is no better time. We should use this opportunity.' Ronnie and Mayank quickly understood the point and concurred. I continued, 'Since all our competitors are not spending, the lead cost will be minimum; we should step up and spend and scale our team. There is no better time to go all out and build the number one brand in higher edtech.' Mayank added, 'I have never seen the university partners in such a stressed state. With all the uncertainty, fees are not getting paid, and they are unable to run the place. For most of these institutions, the money from online coming through us is pretty much the only income. So, we have to step up for their sake too.' That was an angle I had never thought of. There would be no better time to help these universities get inducted into the world of online education. This may mean accelerating changes which otherwise would have taken decades.

Guided by Ronnie's vast experience and insights, we began building the plan to scale upGrad. We repositioned it as a cool upskilling brand and got a new-age agency Womb to work on a brand-new marketing campaign. It was interesting that even with all the Covid-19-related lockdown issues, they were ready to work on our account and figure out a way to shoot an ad which would launch with IPL when IPL 2020 itself was looking hazy. Imagine! But Navin Talreja and Kawal Shoor, co-founders of The Womb, agreed to work personally on the campaign and deliver something amazing.

While the pay cut stayed, we tweaked the same by giving an option to the employees to get the full money back in case we achieved our target for the quarter and make more if we overachieved. This announcement turbocharged the employees who were all aligned towards one revenue objective. Even those without a direct revenue responsibility started asking the revenue team on how they could help them reach the target.

We used this opportunity to double down on ideas like referral and repeat which got our academic, product, technology and mentoring teams aligned indirectly to revenue. All in all, we surged into the Covid-19 wave with the confidence that we were doing our bit to help our customers tide over the wave by upskilling.

While we found our feet to work in this Covid-19-affected world, others in edtech were also going through their own journey. With the lockdown-induced shutting down of schools and coaching centres, most students didn't have any other option but to study with the help of learning apps. Millions thronged the BYJU'S, Vedantu and Unacademy apps which offered free classes that could replace a regular class while their regular teachers were struggling to take video lessons. During the initial days, the traffic went up as high as ten times and we were lucky that the apps and websites didn't crash. With such massive traffic, the confidence of the founders surged and edtech was all over the media as the new way of learning, which was saving the country's students by providing access to education in testing times.

BYJU'S made the best out of the situation by making their app free to everyone and getting huge press coverage for the same. It was a masterstroke by Byju. BYJU'S the learning app was always free for the first fifteen days and post that the app allowed you to access five new videos every month for free, per class. All Byju did was extend the fifteen days to two months, letting kids leverage the product in full when they needed it the most. In normal circumstances, we spend lakhs of rupees every month on Facebook and Google to bring the same kids to our app. Then we spend many more lakhs on emails, SMS services and messaging/engagement/analytics tools to make them use our app but with little success. And here was Byju; with one shrewd decision, he ensured he gave his product to his customers when they wanted it the most and managed the download and engagement literally for free. A few months into the pandemic and lockdown, we used to joke that BYJU'S had a database richer than Aadhaar and that it would no longer need to spend on acquiring users. Such a stroke of brilliance!

When bravehearted founders were creating the narrative of education going the edtech way, governments world over were trying to fight a calamity like never before. The most popular solution employed by the rich nations was monetary easing i.e., central banks flooded the market with money at literally zero interest (in some case even negative), encouraging private investors to invest. Due to the lockdown and fear of Covid-19, the only avenues for investment existed in the digital world, resulting in huge tranches of cheap capital flowing into tech companies. Governments followed this up by handing out cash vouchers to the general public to sustain their livelihood which might have paused due to Covid-19-induced issues. For the spending class to whom the traditional avenues weren't available, this presented a unique situation of excess of liquidity to spend on digital needs. So, all of a sudden, you saw a market for digital where all variables were favourable:

- Investors with cheap capital and only digital companies to invest in
- Customers with excess liquidity and only digital products to spend on
- Competitors with their business obstructed, letting digital counterparts run unchecked

Every single edtech company that was in a position of market leadership found itself in this situation. Though it's debatable how many were able to really convert the customer traffic to actual sales, it was indeed a period of monetary excess.

Typically, in venture investing, an investor values a company at a multiple of its free cash flow—the logic being of paying today for the future money the investor can make from the organization. However, in practice, the valuations are typically done as a multiplier on EBITDA (earnings before interest, tax, depreciation and amortization) since free cash flow calculation is not easy to comprehend and negotiate on. So, an investor who wants to value the company at a multiple of ten on free cash flow will calculate the equivalent on EBITDA as, say, four times and will negotiate on the number. The EBITDA multiplier I'm referring to here is in the context of unlisted start-ups and is not the same as the one we use in stock-market terminology which is basically Enterprise Value/EBITDA.

In recent years, for early-stage companies with high growth and high margins, the conversations have been at a multiplier on revenue. Again, the logic being that these digital companies had 50 per cent EBITDA margin and are growing at 100 per cent year on year and even a valuation today as a multiplier of revenue is as good as the same multiplier on EBITDA next year. So the current valuation is just basis next year's EBITDA and won't make a lot of difference when the opportunity presented is great. Sounds like a great move! The issue is that this 100 per cent growth and 50 per cent margin are all promises and often not lived up to.

Name of the unicorn	Revenue multiples	Name of the unicorn	Revenue multiples
Open Financial Technologies	138.54	Credavenue	19.32
Apna.co	130.59	Oyo	15.27
Spinny	78.00	Licious	14.36
Cred	76.21	Swiggy	13.64
Browserstack	73.92	upGrad	13.52
Globalbees Brands	73.13	ShipRocket	12.29
Sharechat	68.85	Rebel foods	12.04
Groww	66.67	Meesho	11.38
Darwinbox	64.46	Blackbuck	8.97
Lead School	60.59	Moglix	8.93
Onecard	60.39	Mamaearth	8.90
Vedantu	40.14	Dealshare	6.78
Leadsquared	38.88	Acko	6.34
Pine Labs	38.35	PharmEasy	6.07
Curefit	37.18	Fractal	5.94
Purplle	34.30	Car Dekho	5.86
Dailyhunt	33.88	OfBusiness	5.37
Mobile Premier League	32.74	Xpressbees	4.85
BharatPe	32.68	Cars24	4.17
Urban Company	32.17	Zetwerk	3.85
Unacademy	31.77	Games 24x7	3.30
Mensa Brands	30.19	Infra.Market	3.10
Uniphore Software Systems	26.22	ElasticRun	2.85
PhonePe	25.34	Udaan	2.45
PhysicsWallah	20.99	Bigbasket	1.72
Lenskart	19.77	–	–

Indian unicorns and revenue multipliers

Source: Money Control,[12] MCA Filing, Media reports

---

[12] Nikhil Patwardhan and Mansi Verma, 'Indian unicorns sitting on lofty valuations with higher revenue multiples than global peers', 14 February 2023, MoneyControl, https://www.moneycontrol.com/news/business/startup/indian-unicorns-sitting-on-lofty-valuations-with-higher-revenue-multiples-than-global-peers-10076991.html

Since the issue of FEMA (Foreign Exchange Management Act) had come up recently related to start-up funding lately, let us digress a bit and talk about it. The act has its origins in the Licence Raj or Permit Raj era when foreign exchange reserves of our country was meagre and every attempt was made to preserve the dollar. With liberalization, the FEMA too got liberalized but existed because India doesn't have capital account convertibility. Hence it limits the amount of investment an Indian company or individual can make abroad. With start-up funding mostly coming from abroad and the aggressive acquisitions abroad by Indian start-ups, this limit at times gets exceeded. In such circumstances, the company and founders need to take the Reserve Bank of India's (RBI) approval to transfer the dollars. As you can understand, there are controls and paperwork involved, and investors and entrepreneurs who like to move fast don't like such shackles. This is one reason why start-ups were encouraged to establish their holding entity in places like Delaware in the US and Singapore. In fact, Y Combinator stirred up a storm in 2019 and 2020 when they insisted on HQ flipping, i.e., mandatorily asking the companies in its batch to move their headquarters to the US. It is worth saying that Byju is one entrepreneur who didn't entertain the movement of the parent entity to Singapore though there were such requests from some investors. At that point, he told me that he did it out of love for his country and BYJU'S is always going to be an Indian story building the world's largest education company. In hindsight, the decision appears right and with changes in our laws, companies like PhonePe are domiciling back to India from Singapore.

Now coming back to our 'funding surge' situation. Investors with access to the cheap money from Fed's largesse and crazy spike in equity market started investing in edtech in large numbers. It was a period when you could talk to US, Japanese, Chinese, Middle Eastern and European investors in a single day and keep asking for a higher multiplier in every meeting. The biggest beneficiary of this money flow was BYJU'S since it was a market leader by a distance. Just few months previously when I moved out of the company, the organization was closing a round which valued the company at $10 billion and I had felt proud thinking I had joined BYJU'S full-time when it was valued at $100 million and was leaving when the valuation rose 100 times. In a matter of months, I saw my vanity number become history.

Chapter 19

Covid-19 Stage 3: Insanity or FOMO?

Before Covid-19, there were two documented instances of pandemics which killed large parts of the population. The first was Black Death in 1346, a bubonic plague pandemic which killed nearly 200 million people in Eurasia and North Africa. Believed to have originated in the Tian Shan mountains (modern-day border of Kyrgyzstan and China), the bacterium was carried by the Golden Horde during the Mongolian invasion to Crimea and from there, it spread to Europe and North Africa through rats onboard ships which arrived in the Mediterranean. The plague is believed to have halved the human population and post its destruction, driven a resurgent world. In the centuries that followed, the world went through religious, social and economic upheaval leading to Renaissance.

The second pandemic was the Spanish flu of 1918. The spread of information about this pandemic was initially supressed world over to prevent the First World War troops from getting 'demoralized'. However, Spain, a neutral country, allowed the press to freely report about the pandemic and hence the pandemic ended up with the misnomer of Spanish flu. The pandemic of 1918 was caused by an H1N1 virus which triggered an influenza attack among nearly 500 million people, one-third of the world's population then, and killed between 50 million to 100 million people. Here again, coupled with the First World War, this pandemic led to the creation of a new world order.

The World Health Organization estimates that Covid-19 impacted nearly 800 million people and killed nearly 7 million. In terms of the number of deaths and severity, both the earlier pandemics were deadlier than Covid-19. Thanks to the advancement in medical sciences and communication, we had a better response to Covid-19. But the world-changing implications a pandemic brings about held good this time too. Such drastic changes normally change one more thing—the world order.

The Covid-19 fight plan included shutting down life till we invented a cure or at least found ways to curtail and treat it at scale. This approach resulted in scenarios which were not faced by businesses ever before 2020. So, when schools and coaching classes shut down and students moved to online learning en masse, what should an investor who is responsible for chasing the trend do?

This is the question which started the race for investing in the market leaders of edtech. Since demand was more than supply and lead indicators, i.e., traffic surge, indicated a future where edtech could replace schools and colleges, the valuation chased the hypothesis. If you think back, this is exactly what happened with the dot-com bubble (or dot-com boom). The Internet was replacing everything—libraries, shopping, newspapers, etc. Investors used traffic and eyeballs as the lead indicator to revenue to value internet companies. Lot of dud companies with no clear business models did IPOs or raised venture funding at sky-high valuations. There were even infamous swaps like AT&T and AOL. Eventually, most of these investments bit the dust sucking out billions of investor money. The impact was all the more catastrophic because the investors during the dot com phase were not just institutional; lot of retail investors also lost their money since some of these companies were listed, resulting in a social shock more than economic one. Those few months of free fall is famous today as dot com bust.

People have the habit of bashing this story as recklessness. Take a step back and see how we do things today. We have stopped working on paper and its Microsoft Office or Google docs we use all the time. We have stopped going to libraries for our research; we google. We shop for most of our needs on Amazon. The thesis that digital economy will replace the traditional economy in the future has actually happened. Where people went wrong were the companies—pets.com, epidemic. com and computers.com died because they never had a solid business model not because people went back to physical stores en mass leaving online. However, it is undeniable that the larger trend reading was right and hence no institutional investor (VC, PE, hedge funds, etc.) would have lost money betting on this trend. It is a similar scenario which got repeated in 2020 and it was the key performance indicator of the investors to spot the trend and put money into companies leading the new trends. They really wouldn't have cared about giving a higher multiplier in the fear of missing out. Worrying about a few millions here or there especially when they had access to cheap capital was definitely not prudent when the question was about owning a piece of the future.

During the period September 2020 to September 2021, there was a mad rush of capital which chased Indian edtech firms. There were large VCs who missed out on these companies in the early days but desperately wanted a piece of the pie now.

With the doubling and tripling of traffic, they were also ready to increase the multiplier enjoyed by these companies. BYJU'S valuation, which was close to $10 billion in May 2020, went up to $12 billion in November 2020 and then to $17 billion by November 2021. In July 2022, they hit a $22 billion valuation. Literally, the valuation doubled in two years (2020 to 2022) and the company became the most valued edtech in the world and most valued start-up in India. Similarly, Unacademy raised at $400 million in February 2020 raised money again in September 2020 at $1.4 billion and then at $1.93 billion in November 2020 and quite unbelievably at $3.42 billion in August 2021. Notably, the big increase in valuation happened when two funds entered the cap table—SoftBank and Tiger Capital. Known to be super aggressive and extremely successful, both these funds had a huge reputation in being prophetic with their investment and it seemed like they saw India's education landscape completely changing soon. This was also a period when large Chinese funds like Tencent and top PEs like BlackRock, T. Rowe Price, etc. started betting on Indian start-ups. All these gave a lot of credibility to these companies and the sector. The period of September 2020 to September 2021 was also a phase of exuberance in financial markets. Every rich country—US, Japan, Western Europe—had brought down their interest rates to zero and was handing out cash in some cases to people to prevent a crash. The markets had rebounded and were going through a phase of accelerating price to earning ratios. Even with not much physical economic activity, money was everywhere.

At upGrad, we were busy with our repositioning and marketing exercise. Post the announcement of lockdowns, IPL 2020 was indefinitely suspended but trade believed that it would happen sometime in September. We knew that would be our opportunity and were working our campaigns to hit that timeline. This meant that we needed to create, plan and shoot our ad film during the Covid-19 pandemic. With the help of technology and a great team, we were able to cruise through the process. After debating a lot on if we needed a celebrity like every other edtech (Shahrukh Khan [BYJU'S], Dhoni [Unacademy], Aamir Khan [Vedantu], Virat Kohli [Great Learning], etc.), our agency was able to present an idea which we felt encapsulated what we stood for—upskilling formal courses which would get you industry-ready.

We researched multiple themes and finally picked up office politics and the chemistry between the employee and boss as the premise of our ad. The story was a play on the adage 'chaatna' or sucking up to your boss, a common phenomenon at the workplace. The story was a funny take on the premise by literally picturing the boss as a donkey. After talking to thousands of our customers, we felt that upskilling post finding a job is no longer something only geeks do and the modern-day working professional needs it to make their jobs exciting, which happens when you do something you are skilled in.

Indians are adept at learning our jobs while doing it. However, the process is inefficient, and one ends up taking the painful route of trial and error while getting there. It normally takes multiple iterations and projects to achieve mastery by self-learning, going through documentation, learning from colleagues and learning by trying it out. In the process, usually the learning is slow and prone to error. In the fast-paced world of today, it's very common for technology to change by the time one learns it. Hence the simple question was why make it slow and painful by trying to learn your job in an unstructured manner, i.e., while doing it. Instead learn the tools that will help you do your job better in a structured way, first, and then apply those to the job to be successful quickly. This is the premise the upskilling business is built on and what we wanted to communicate to our TG.

Thanks to lockdown-induced constraints, the ad shoot was not something we could do in India then. So upGrad's donkey ad became one of the first ads to be shot remotely with the director and creative team sitting in Mumbai and controlling the entire shoot which happened in Estonia (a country in Europe) on a Zoom call. I was amazed at how perfect it turned out—technology had, indeed, come a long way.

Alongside a marketing overhaul, we were working hard on our product. We knew that the pandemic was one opportunity for us to prove that the online medium works as good or even better with regard to education. To do that we had to deliver outcomes which only happens when learners learn the skills. So, we added multiple new features to our learning experience on a war footing. With the help of our university partners, we replicated every point of learning in a university system online—live lectures, recorded pre-read, group projects, case studies (which had to be analysed in groups and submitted). Let me explain the underlying thought process for these features.

There are two key aspects of education which drive learning—discipline and community. The essence of a structured curriculum is to drive discipline. A teacher in class, deadlines of assignments and project submissions, regular exams which take place at a prerequisite date—all of these drive discipline in students, thus making learning possible in a planned time duration. An engaging instructor and interesting content make the discipline-driving part easier by making things exciting and driving the internal sources of motivation of students.

The second aspect is community. Most of us learn well in groups and from our peers. One reason why modern-day

MBA programmes focus so much on group projects, case study discussions in class, etc. is this. A desi version of the same can be seen in our coaching capital Kota where real learning happens late night every day when students sit together to solve daily practice problems (DPPs). The same happens the night before exams in engineering college hostels when students sit around their 'exam-buddy' (an otherwise unpopular kid who becomes the darling a day before exams) for gyaan to cross the barrier the next day. Our efforts at upGrad were to replicate these two aspects online to make the learning happen and thus deliver outcomes.

We built several features to make these happen. Some ended up becoming quite successful while others didn't get much traction. One feature which got traction during Covid-19 was networking—students could network with other students in their batch and alumni, taking the community feature to another level. We felt such informal interactions are important and a lot of learning happens if these are done well. We were trying to ensure that every aspect of learning and outcomes which a learner experienced in a high-quality university was available online too, especially during Covid-19 when there was no way to go learn in campuses. We also increased the frequency of our buddy interactions with learners, a key reason why our engagement was high.

Learning online alongside your job is not easy. There will be hundreds of reasons to bunk or fall behind—a project deadline, party with friends, family time, kids' exams, someone ill at home or even a partner who asks for a lot of your time. Amidst all this, finding a couple of hours every day to study, submit assignments, take exams and do all this for a period of one to two years is not easy. We realized it early on and invented the concept of buddy. A buddy is a learner's partner in his/her online learning journey. The buddy tracks the learner's progress and ensures the learner follows the learning schedule. The buddy is constantly in touch with the learner and reaches out if classes are missed or assignments are not submitted in time. In this manner, a buddy replicates the peer effect and parent effect which helps most learners to successfully complete the course. During Covid-19, we saw that a buddy ended up being a friend to our learners and in a lot of cases provided the emotional support which learners craved for when they were stuck at home with cobwebs of uncertainty in their mind.

Thanks to a series of steps taken, we were able to convert a substantial part of the increased traffic into business and then put all our focus on ensuring every one of those who took our courses got the outcomes they were looking for. We were always clear that if our customers went through a life-changing experience with our course, they would take care of our future business. This was the simple philosophy which propelled our business. Numbers followed the effort and upGrad was also able to leverage the existing good sentiments on edtech to raise money. This was significant because till then high ed was not a segment VCs were interested in. The segment was always seen as low TAM and with high regulatory risk. With the changing environment, these negatives disappeared, and upskilling started being looked upon as a high-growth segment.

Chapter 20

The New Normal, Second Wave and the Rise of Motivators

After two months of intense lockdown, things started opening up slowly from 8 June. The normalization process took a few months with constraints still in place, such as negative RT-PCR test for travel and strict masking norms. Surviving through constant changes in the ecosystem is hard for both an established company and a budding start-up. It's a testimony to the resilience of the entrepreneurs and the team they lead that we all survived.

Historically, edtech has been a high-attrition industry because of the way it has evolved. Especially in the B2C model, there was a lot of sales push involved because of the nature of the product and the expectations of high growth. Edtech was not alone in this. A similar situation exists in banking, financial services and insurance (BFSI), especially insurance and banking product sales as well. All these sectors are scourged by high attrition which has prevented the models from maturing and stabilizing.

The outcome of high attrition is that you are perpetually hiring, training and working with a young sales force. During Covid-19, we found it quite challenging to do the training and integration of new hires within the company's culture, remotely. Traditionally, a newbie apprentice learns a lot of finer things about the job through informal conversations with his team. It is when they sit together and help each other out that they become close as a team and start working towards a shared objective. It is this aspect which went missing the most when the world started working from home. While we were one of the first to pivot online driving productivity while working from home, we were also one of the first to call certain teams back to office when we were not able to take productivity to the level we wanted. Thus started the new normal of hybrid mode, with few teams coming to office intermittently. These ideas are not easy to implement especially when you are a young manager with an inexperienced team of freshers distributed across office and their homes. A large part of your time is just spent on meetings where you struggle to make your point heard through the digital curtains. In spite of all these struggles, people rose up to the challenge and the learning continued.

The Second Wave

The year 2021 started with a lot of hope since the data showed that infection had peaked and subsided. The world welcomed 2021 with enthusiasm and then the second wave struck. If the first wave of Covid-19 in May 2020 was a shock and struggle, the second one in March 2021 was disastrous. The scenario was spooky due to the pace at which the mutated virus impacted a person's respiratory system resulting in death. India's rickety healthcare infrastructure started collapsing under the impact of the quick pace of infections. Running offices was impossible during this phase and so was asking our team members from distant locations to return home. Hence was born our model of providing accommodation to employees coming to office. We negotiated deals to move our employees to hotels where they could stay and work safely while following all the Covid-19 protocols. Hotels like Royal Orchid in Bengaluru and Hyatt in Mumbai became our partners in upskilling our customers. This system again was extremely hard to work, and all kudos to Deepak—our sales head—and his team for making it happen. They systematically went about defining processes which allowed them to track productivity at a granular level and implemented multiple team-building activities.

'This is becoming a hostel and slowly the chill mode is setting in,' Deepak reported in our weekly reviews. 'Your team's productivity is good and costs are under control. I don't want to do the complete flip-flop of going back to work from home now only to shift back to office when it reopens in a few weeks,' I responded. 'That's true. The biggest enemy of our work is disruption and we have to do everything to make the counsellor and manager feel no changes happens in their daily work,' Deepak agreed and went about continuously tweaking processes and review mechanisms to ensure the team felt charged and had clarity every day to deliver output.

While online learning was adjusting and delivering to the new normal, there were large parts of traditional education which were struggling with this once-in-their-lifetime emergency. Schools—small and big—were being forced to conduct their lecturers online. Most of the teachers who had no experience teaching in front of a screen were asked to take their classes in front of their basic smart phone and without a board and students they were used to for years. Imagine the plight of a math teacher who had to make slides for her algebra class. She would have struggled with the math symbols which had to be inserted through an unfriendly user interface of PowerPoint. If teachers were struggling so much, what would be the fate of the students? All of the sudden, every kid and teacher was searching online for videos which helped them understand concepts and using those instead of making it themselves. This also increased the demand for teachers who were proficient in taking classes online.

While schools survived due to the formal nature of the institution, coaching centres were in a worse situation. To prevent gatherings and crowds, the government banned coaching classes from conducting physical classes. As a result, this low-margin business which survived on immediate cash flows started sinking into deep trouble. India's famed coaching factory Kota shut down and the drama around helping students to return home during the lockdown gave the entire place a further bad image as if the existing bad PR was not enough.

Two trends emerged out of all this:

Rise of the Motivators: Every young teacher moved online to create a following for themselves on YouTube because edtech companies trying to take up the space of Kota coaching were ready to pay them crores if they could prove their online following, measured in the number of YouTube followers, was high. The easiest way for a teacher to draw followers is by conducting motivational lectures rather than complex JEE or NEET content. Motivation is about giving gyaan of success with no context or accountability and was easy to digest for students. Teachers also found their own niches by doing these lectures in Hindi and local languages. Students who were young enough to be misled ended up drinking this kool-aid in the name of online education, and followership started building. Along with hours and hours of motivation also came drama. Individuals who called themselves teachers or education influencers started joking, screaming and in some cases even abusing to win followers and association with edtech firms for a hefty package. In some cases, they started building their own edtech companies.

Consolidation in Coaching Industry: The decades-old coaching industry started consolidating. Large players like Allen and Aakash started looking for partners who could capitalize them and help them survive in testing times. The small and medium ones which could not take the pressure any more simply started shutting down. More about coaching industries later.

Consolidation in Education

One of the biggest gifts Byju has is his ability to spot a trend much before anyone else can in the industry. While everyone was talking about how online was going to eat up all offline versions of learning, he correctly predicted how the trend would reverse after the world opened up post pandemic. Hence, he was keen on buying a large coaching company which would help him provide coaching to students even when they moved away from online. This was not a lack of confidence in online, rather the astuteness of his understanding that the customer has the freedom to choose the medium at will and that there will be a captive audience for all mediums over time, like e-commerce will never end retail; they will always exist in tandem.

Leveraging the great run during Covid-19 and his ability to raise money, Byju began focusing on acquiring companies in the adjacent segments which would help him be a full-service player in education. His acquisition of Aakash in 2021 in a nearly $1-billion deal was definitely the best among the lot. This can be compared to Amazon's acquisition of Whole Foods. The increase in the value of Amazon stocks after the news of the deal started spreading was enough to pay for the $14 billion value of Whole Foods. This was because Whole Foods fits seamlessly with Amazon or the market believed so and provided one more avenue to Amazon Prime customers. Because Byju could command such a huge multiplier during Covid-19, his cost of capital used for buying Aakash was nothing compared to the value the organization brought to BYJU'S. The best part was that he also gave a very good value to the founders and investors of Aakash and didn't try to take advantage of the bad situation they were in due to the pandemic. He continued his buying spree and bought more companies to complete the full spectrum—Great Learning in higher ed, Epic for reading in kids, and Tynker and WhiteHat Jr to help children learn coding skills.

Other big edtechs followed suit. While Unacademy acquired a slew of smaller companies such as PrepLadder, TapChief and WiFiStudy, Vedantu acquired Instasolv, a doubt-clearing app, and Deeksha, an offline coaching centre quite popular across Karnataka. In higher ed, upGrad acquired KnowledgeHut, Insofe and Impartus, among others. The activity around coaching didn't end with just edtech acquisitions. The other large coaching player, Allen, diluted its equity to a newly minted venture fund called Bodhi Tree. The vision was to create Allen Digital, a digital version of Allen Academy which would replicate Allen's methodology that produced hundreds of top JEE rankers online. This is the same direction Aakash was also taking in partnership with BYJU'S. As we came closer to the end of the pandemic, it was becoming increasingly clear that everyone was behind this new fictitious concept called hybrid learning.

Chapter 21

India's Coaching Factories and Indians' Aspirations Abroad

By 5 a.m., the locality was buzzing with activity. The eateries were ready to serve breakfast and groups of students could be seen sipping steaming tea by the roadside, trying to gear up for the day. Gigantic hoardings with life-size images of teachers overlooked the streets announcing the credibility of various coaching centres and how they can help them crack the competitive exam. By 7 a.m., students all looking the same in their formal attire were rushing for their 8 a.m. classes; some busy going through their notes making sure they utilize the last moment, probably before a test scheduled that day.

This is not a scene from Kota, the Mecca of JEE coaching like some of you would have thought. This is the daily morning routine from Rajendar Nagar in Delhi, the hub of UPSC coaching in India. Students from all across the country turn up here to prepare for the 'legendary' exam which can make them part of the steel frame of India—the Indian Administrative Service. However, your guess is not far off. The scenes are close to what happens in Kota every morning. Whether it is Rajendar Nagar in Delhi (UPSC) or Kota in

Rajasthan (JEE) or Mylapore in Chennai, Tamil Nadu (CA), the scenes and life are quite similar. Lakhs of students come to these coaching factories from towns all across the country to prepare for various competitive exams. They live in paying guest accommodations and hostels in the area and are expected to only study all the time though that's hardly the case. You will even meet people who have been living there and preparing for five-plus years. Imagine spending six years trying to crack an exam (JEE) which admits one to a four-year course. The stress, the peer and societal pressure you will encounter on these streets is unimaginable.

Kota was always famous among the science students in high school. However, the fame, more precisely notoriety, touched its zenith with all the negative PR during the lockdown and the YouTube series *The Kota Factory*. Kota became the emblem of all the things good and bad about competitive exam coaching in India. In my view, it's rather unfair to look at Kota as a representative of India's coaching industry. Coaching in India is an estimated Rs 58,000 crore market which is contributed to by thousands of coaching companies, individual teachers and platforms—big and small—all across the country. Kota is a hub for JEE coaching which is dominated today by one player—Allen Career Institute. The estimated size of the Kota market will be around 2300 crore (1.3 lakh ARPU and 1.75 lakh students).

Coaching began in Kota with V.K. Bansal, who started coaching class XI and XII students for JEE in 1985. He was an engineer from Banaras Hindu University (now IIT Banaras) who used to work in one of the industries of the once-bustling industrial town. Bansal was diagnosed with muscular dystrophy in 1974 which left him paralysed eventually. Rather than being upset about his physical state and subsequent loss of employment due to the demise of industry in Kota, he built a new career for himself in coaching. It is said that when he started teaching kids for JEE using his unique structured approach, the entire batch could sit around his dining table. Everything changed when the first batch of students cracked the JEE exam with top ranks and Bansal promptly set up Bansal Classes in 1991. Though it was not the first coaching institute in the country, it used to get disproportionate results thanks to the unique methods Bansal introduced. Along with an intense, interesting and deep coverage of the JEE curriculum in a scheduled manner, he had one tool which in my view propelled his results—daily practice problems, or DPP.

DPP was a sheet of JEE-level problems given every day after class, covering the portions covered that day. The genius of this tool is how it stirred up both discipline and community in learning. Since Bansal made it a point to check every day if the problems were done and discuss the doubts the next day, kids were forced to learn, revise and apply the concepts they learned the same day—a critical success point in JEE preparation. The discipline ensured they learned the vast topics in a structured manner and kept building on what they knew. But it didn't end there. DPPs were also hard and so naturally students came together in the evening after class to solve it together creating a community working together to crack JEE. A community is a very important aspect of learning. One of the reasons why a Montessori way of learning is able to drive learning much faster than traditional teaching (teacher lecturing to several students) is the community it develops in open classrooms where kids are allowed to work on activities together to learn. B-schools try to do community learning through case study groups and project cohorts. Whether or not Bansal was aware, his DPP developed a sense of community. The classes brought his students together and they helped each other in the learning process.

Rankers and Bankers

The genius of Bansal and Kota didn't end with the teaching model. They knew that grabbing top ranks was the most critical thing to their business. They were also aware that other institutes across the country would quickly copy their teaching model. So, building the top-rank moats meant creating a system which would ensure that every year top ranks came to them. Thus was born the rankers-batch model. In this, the coaching centre scouts for talented students in high school who have the potential to score top ranks in JEE. These students, once identified through a vast network from across the country, are brought to Kota and trained by the best faculty in the institutes free of cost. A combination of talent and right mentoring ensures that these students reach where they were supposed to get to. The model was so successful that for several years, Kota factories dominated the top ranks in JEE. This hegemony continues till today except for the brief hiatus due to Hyderabad's integrated schooling factories in the middle. As is seen from the results, the rankers model became so successful that soon people started calling Kota classes the 'Rankers and Bankers' model. Rankers get it all free and get the ranks while the rest of the students who take admissions seeing the ranks pay for their coaching.

Bansal's success created clones like Allen, Resonance, etc. which were started by break-away teachers or old students at the institute. Today, Kota gets an estimated 1.75 lakh students every year. The market is currently dominated by Allen, which is said to own nearly 70 per cent of the students or 1.25 lakh admissions. Coaching and competition run everything in the town—from rickshaw-walas who gets paid a commission if he 'delivers' the admission, to hostels which ensure comfortable accommodation for students from certain institutes, and teachers who can get paid in crores if they are popular. However, Kota is not alone in this kind of life and competition. A student's experience at Vajiram & Ravi in Rajinder Nagar for UPSC or at Narayana Integrated Schools in Hyderabad for JEE is no different. Similar pressures and burden of expectations weigh on them through their days in these coaching factories.[13]

Historically, coaching developed in India due to the large demand–supply gap which existed in India's premier institutions and courses—IITs, medical colleges, NITs, UPSC, CA, etc. This imbalance, along with multiple state syllabi followed across the country, led to the creation of entrance exams. These exams were conducted by various state or central education departments and followed the same Class XI and XII syllabus in case of engineering and medicine exams. In practice, the questions papers set often required graduate-level knowledge and high-level application skills to crack and gain admission to these sought-after portals of higher education. Schools and colleges often fell short of the quality required to train students for these exam papers and thus emerged coaching centres—a new breed

---

[13] Devina Sengupta, 'Inside the cut-throat battle for Kota: Unacademy vs Allen', 12 July 2022, Mint, https://www.livemint.com/education/news/inside-the-cut-throat-battle-for-kota-unacademy-vs-allen-11657559737505.html

TN Education Desk, 'Kota Coaching centre makes it to Guinness Book of records with 1.27 lakh registered students', 18 January 2023, https://www.timesnownews.com/education/kotas-allen-coaching-sets-record-of-highest-number-of-students-in-a-coaching-institute-article-97096494#:~:text=in%20a%20city.-

of institutions which followed a structured curriculum and rigorous discipline to help students crack these papers.

For most of the students in India from my generation, getting into these premium institutions was life changing. It offered them and their family a legitimate and quick route out of poverty and at times a middle-class existence. Hence, when coaching centres offered a way out, parents were ready to grab them with both hands. Money started flowing in and with it the industry flourished. Most of the coaching institutes were started by a teacher who then expanded by hiring more teachers. This model though extremely successful at their base location has proved unsuccessful when they tried to scale nationally. There are many examples like Bansal Classes and IITian PACE which couldn't scale beyond their core location and hence ended up creating coaching factories—small towns like Kota where students had to come to study in their institutes. Incredible but true; doesn't it sound a bit like the adage: 'If the mountain won't come to Mohammed, Mohammed will have to go to the mountain'? The issue of scale which they faced is not new and you see this a lot in owner-managed companies. Scale comes with focus on processes and decentralization of decision-making. Owners with specific skill sets drive largely based on their personal charisma which overrules processes in most cases. A lot of founders in India, including some of the education and coaching entrepreneurs, realized this and ensured their next generation was trained at the best institutions possible to professionalize management. Either through the next generation or by bringing in professionals from outside, professional management is essential to support a company in its scaling journey. Ceding control at the right juncture is key in the larger interest of the company.

Post Covid-19, edtech companies entered the offline coaching business and started trying to disrupt the fifty-year-old business with technology, or at least that's what they are claiming to do. We will have to wait and watch to understand how edtech companies are going to make money in the low-margin coaching business even when they will need to pay teachers more, make the centres swankier and charge students competitive fees. While some of them have built swanky centres, others have wisely decided to acquire established players for operational excellence—a key skill for success in this hyper-competitive space. The latter approach has created an interesting outcome. All of a sudden, there are large coaching centres which are run by professional managers with promoters ceding control. This has the potential of moving this industry to scale, just like it happened with other sectors in India. I won't be surprised if Aakash Institute, the best example in this sector, will go on to create the first truly all-India coaching network. At least they will allow lakhs of students to prepare for JEE and NEET while living with their parents and in active contact with their friends rather than in the high-pressure Kota factory away from a safe and supporting family environment.

Changing Aspirations

The number of students writing JEE and NEET increased by nearly 20 per cent in last couple of years. So, we can safely assume that this market is not slowing down. However, for the new generation exposed to the internet and the world at large, these tests are no longer the be all and end all of their lives. Increasingly, kids today are taking up professions which they feel is a natural fit for them. This has resulted in subjects like commerce and law gaining traction. But the biggest change, thanks to the exposure, has been the huge growth in students who want to go abroad and study. In 2022 alone, 7.7 lakh Indian students went abroad to study and immigrate to a better lifestyle. Most of them were people who were not successful at getting into their desired institutions or courses through these super-tough competitive exams. Ten years ago, they might have destroyed their life repeating Kota several times, but not any more. Today, they are looking at several private options in India and abroad and deciding between these. The biggest reason for this change is the cost of education. While education at IITs, NITs and various government medical colleges has become more and more expensive every year, the cost of studying abroad has fallen thanks to vacant seats in universities abroad and innovative products launched by edtech companies offering study abroad. Today, it's possible to study abroad at almost half the cost as earlier because of a unique credit transfer model where students can complete their first year or first two years online while in India and the rest on campus abroad. This means the student doesn't spend at regular offline rates when they are learning online nor incur the living expenditure while doing the online part of the course, resulting in huge savings. Several such models along with modern private schools are making it possible for students to look beyond the glamour of premier institutions. There is no doubt that these trends will gain strength and no student in India will be deprived of quality and stress-free education.[14]

---

[14] Jyoti Yadav, 'India's Tuition Republic is bigger than ever. Coaching culture is an epidemic now' 19 December 2022, ThePrint, https://theprint.in/features/indias-tuition-republic-is-bigger-than-ever-coaching-culture-is-an-epidemic-now/1270638/

Chapter 22

NEP: India's Revolutionary Higher Education Stack

The India Stack is the digital infrastructure which enables the government and businesses to deliver services to the population presence-less, paperless and cashless, with their consent. This project which has been in the works for nearly a decade, started with Aadhaar which was then used to do eKYC, followed by eSign. Both eKYC and eSign drastically helped in reducing the administrative hassles and cost involved in the same incurred by businesses. The next one, UPI, which allowed lightning-fast payments was the real game changer; this time for the consumer too since government made the transaction cost zero, effectively making most of the country cashless. Currently, the Stack is bringing in documents of identity and credibility from various government institutions into one database called DigiLocker. India Stack is the world's largest Open API system and is revolutionizing our lives in ways we had never imagined.

The new NEP is the education version of the India Stack and it's ambition is to give the power of education to the learner rather than the institutions. At the very heart of it, NEP restructures the school system from a 10 + 2 to 5 + 3 + 3 + 4 system, bringing more focus to critical thinking and outcomes. Though it looks at bringing in lot of interesting ideas in school education, it is in higher education that the policy becomes truly revolutionary. Let's look at some of the ideas in the policy which will solve for access, affordability and quality:

- Establishment of multidisciplinary higher educational institutions (HEIs) with more than 3000 students in every district of the country.
- Bringing in flexibility by allowing exit from a degree course. A student can drop off from a three-year graduation course after year one with a certificate, year two with a diploma and get a degree if he/she completes all three years.
- Learners who opt for four-year graduation courses can complete their master's in one year and have the option to enrol for PhD directly after graduation.
- Online degrees and ODL get the same level of credibility with exact same degree/diploma certificate with a citation on the back about the mode of learning. Quality is controlled by only allowing HEIs with proven track record determined by their NIRF (National Institute Ranking Framework) ranking or NAAC (National Assessment and Accreditation Council) rating to give out online and ODL degrees.
- Allowing industry professionals with deep experience in their domain to work as Professors of Practice at HEIs, thus allowing deeper industry interfacing.

These elements of flexibility can allow students in a country like ours to finally take up education in parallel with the jobs they are forced to take up to help their families, soon after schooling.

I see this as a great enabler and hence when online degrees were announced as part of the NEP 2020 (central government budget 2020), upGrad was the first edtech to plunge into it and start discussions with universities in NIRF top 100 to launch an online degree programme. With our years of experience in online education, we were sure that we could help in making the delivery a success because as against the popular perception, online education was not taking classes in front of a Zoom screen. That way, you will be down to zero attendance in no time and outcomes which is such an important aspect of NEP will never be achieved. We had learned this first-hand, and our tech platform and allied services were exactly what these institutions should be using to make the online degrees a success. Else online degrees will meet the same fate as distance learning where the inferior quality is keeping corporates away from giving the ODL students the same level of credibility as a full-time regular student.

Our effort with reach-out and discussions with multiple universities didn't make much headway since either they felt edtech was not necessary or they themselves were not sure how to go about it considering few grey areas in regulation.

'I don't need upGrad to sell degrees with this logo,' the director of a legendary IIT said pointing at the institute logo above his head. This was the one-line response to my passionate presentation on how upGrad can be a great partner to the august institute in their effort to launch online degrees. Our pitch was to become the partner which can provide all the services (tech platform, marketing, mentoring and customer service, to name a few) as allowed by regulation while they focused on curriculum and delivery. Not in a mood to accept defeat that easily, I responded, 'I agree, professor; all you have to say is JEE is not required for admissions, and you will have a deluge of applicants. But that's not where we can be of help. We understand how learners can be engaged and kept excited through this lonely journey of online learning. Our platform is world-class and developed by putting in all these nuances. The results are there for you to see. Almost 89 per cent of our learners complete the course and 80 per cent says they got outcomes.' The director smiled and raised his hand signalling me to stop. 'I am happy at the work you are doing in India and the tech you have developed. However, we won't partner with anyone for degrees. We are more than happy to partner with you for certificates. There are multiple other angles to it. We have developed our own platform for online delivery in SWAYAM and we want to invest and improve it to bring it to the levels of edtechs like you. Also, I'm dealing here with some of the brightest students and alumni, and partnership with a private company and offering degrees online doesn't go down well with them.'

My interactions with professors in India's top universities—IITs, IIMs, IIITs, NITs, etc.—have always been some of the best intellectual conversations I've had in my life. However, they were all bound by hundreds of constraints which prevented them from opening their premier courses to online media. I strongly believe that we are doing gross injustice by not making the teaching talent in these temples of learning accessible to the whole world through online. The faculty has always argued with me at this point saying that the National Programme on Technology Enhanced Learning (NPTEL) is doing exactly this by giving access to the work by these professors to anyone who has a computer and internet access. And this is where I always tell them online learning is not giving access to some videos or live streaming. It's fundamentally about replicating the moments of learning through multiple tools available to a top university, like projects, case studies, simulations, group learning, peer learning, best teachers, mentoring, etc, online. NPTEL provides one element—recorded classes from great teachers. If documented information like recordings were enough to learn, there was no need for universities; libraries would have been sufficient.

One of the IITs soon went ahead and started an online bachelor's programme that allowed students to enrol without JEE. As the director rightly said, they enrolled over 8000 students in the first batch without any marketing. End of year two, 101 students from the batch received a provisional diploma. That's a big drop from the original number, though the real number of students passing out will only be known by the end of year three.

NEP in higher ed got a big push due to the closing down of physical classes as a result of the Covid-19 lockdown. The government didn't want the academic year to be wasted and hence eased the constraints on top universities to launch online degrees. This helped us to convince top private universities to partner with us and do online degrees to help students. There was huge data available that the market was waiting for something like this. Every year, in India, more than 10 lakh students enrol for distance learning degrees. Why do so many students enrol for something like distance learning which doesn't even enjoy high credibility in the job market? The reason is simple—there are lakhs and lakhs of Indians who want to learn and take a degree but can't do that due to the lack of flexibility.

I have always believed that making a good product is not enough in India. In a country this complex, it is important to pass the message about your product far and wide so that the lesser-informed denizens understand how it can change their life and start consuming it. This is the reason why we always stress on the right marketing dose behind everything we launch. The same was done with degree courses. While the campaign was very popular with the students and the number and spread of enrolment were a testimony to the same, it didn't really strike a chord with the academia and government.

When you are in education, it is important to be understand every stakeholder's perspective and be grounded, and this is what we learned and did. We innovated newer mediums of marketing to spread the message which was amenable to all stakeholders and ensured that the message of online degrees as a way to earn a degree for those who hadn't done so due to the lack of flexibility, spread sufficiently.

In 2021–22, 72,400 students enrolled for online degrees with Indian universities of which 54,000 were taking online degrees from private and deemed-to-be universities. This number was less than 26,000 in 2020–21, clearly showing how fast this medium was becoming acceptable to students and parents. Two years of efforts from edtech and private universities have also given the government a lot of confidence today to work on a Central Digital University (CDU). There are obviously questions about whether this proposed CDU will go the IGNOU way and end up creating lakhs of online degrees which do not have much value in the market. I really hope this doesn't happen and the government continues working with edtechs to build the CDU.

Another positive and unexpected development of things moving online has been the changes in ODL. With online platforms becoming an integral part of universities, ODL courses also started getting digitalized, improving the quality. Today literally these online degrees and ODL degrees can be taken by anyone with a basic smart phone and a decent internet connection. We have scores of students from traditionally backward states (in terms of education access) like (former) Jammu and Kashmir and the North-east studying with UpGrad. ODL admissions grew to 14 lakh in 2020–21 and 20 lakh in 2021–22.

With all this growth in numbers, a question that haunted our minds all through our hectic days during the pandemic was: 'Will we be able to retain all these people online once their offices and universities open?' We didn't have to wait for long to find out!

Chapter 23

Opening Up: Back to Reality

When we experienced the Covid-19-induced pick up in learners, we knew that this was a period given to us online players to show that we could deliver outcomes like any offline university. So, all efforts were only on one thing—outcomes.

Unlike the West where people go to universities to acquire knowledge and create a better version of themselves, education in India has always been about a life-transformational experience. That is, one's life should get transformed into a better one economically after the completion of education, which typically happens with a better job. So, there is only one objective of education in India—job, better job or a new job. We survey every student who comes to us on this aspect and have realized that this doesn't always mean a new job in a different company. Lot of working professionals just want to move ahead in the same organization, either in the same profile or a different profile. It is this understanding that helped us improve the way we delivered our courses—recognizing the shortcomings in learners which were holding them back from reaching their destination and then working on the same to make it happen.

It is because we were able to deliver outcomes at this scale that when the lockdown ended, we didn't see any drop in our customers. The same can't be said about a lot of other segments in edtech. For companies working in test prep, the outcome is getting a top rank in one of the entrance exams—JEE or NEET. However, through 2020 and 2021, though there were lakhs of students who learned online for these exams, there were hardly any success stories from among them. The top ranks were from the traditional institutes of Aakash and Allen. This is the reason why Kota, in spite of all the negative PR, experienced a surge in demand the moment it reopened. Allen claimed 1.2 lakh-plus admissions in 2022, a record in Kota and double the number from their previous best of 66,000. Aakash has grown spectacularly post BYJU'S acquisition and opening up. Test prep was the most impacted category for edtech with the end of the pandemic and opening up, and the reason is quite obvious—Aakash got literally all of the top 50 NEET ranks and Allen got 47 out of top 100 JEE advanced ranks last year. If online is replacing coaching centres, where are the results? Out of the online players only Vendantu was able to capture a few ranks in the top 100 for JEE in an otherwise disappointing performance by online players. The learning for us in this is obvious: we cannot make products and leave it to fate that students will learn. Education, especially education online, needs to be a rigorous and highly planned delivery process to drive results.

In the K-10 and tuition market again, while students have returned to offline tuition centres, online has firmly parked itself as a mainstream alternative. In 2023, we will see these two segments fight it out to give the best to the customer, quite similar to how e-commerce and retail are fighting it out. Here again, delivery will be the king. It's for edtech to use the innovative tools they have at their disposal and weave a magical delivery to drive results. In K-10 especially, there is no one national-level exam to crack, so edtech efficacy will be measured against the marks the students score in their schools and Class X boards. So, the platform will have to train the student for being successful at their schools.

The biggest casualty of the opening up were the start-up valuations established during the pandemic and the associated burn which was going in full throttle to generate bookings (gross revenue) to justify these valuations. The music stopped and traffic dropped! A lot of this traffic was not from the economically strong customers and hence would have never converted at the price points the companies were selling. As a result, not much of revenue scaling would have come from spending the large amount of money raised resulting in a critical situation where these companies needed urgent cash to keep the business running.

I had always believed that there will be a crash and a mild recession post Covid-19 opening up. I reasoned that since all these investments had happened in the private markets and insulated from the public markets; the loss will not impact the general public at large like dot com crash. However, the fall of the Silicon Valley Bank (SVB) and subsequent incidents belied my assessment. SVB crashed because they mismanaged investment of burgeoning deposits which flowed to their coffers during good days of start-up investment in 2020–2021. Seeking higher returns, the bank dramatically increased the holding of long-term securities. The securities crashed after the Fed increased rates in the post Covid-19 period. High Fed rates also created a challenging funding environment for start-ups and the clients started pulling out their money for liquidity. Crunched for funds, SVB sold the securities at lower price in a bad market. The information on these led to a bank run. Sorry for the slight digression but I can't stop myself from saying this can never happen in India because the strict RBI policies on cash reserve ratio and statutory liquidity ratio ensure that the banks always have cash and can never invest all their money in market instruments. This is good in bad times like this but bad in good times when the banks miss the opportunity to make a killing with all that cheap cash sitting with them.

In start-up lexicon, the safety of a start-up is measured by runway, i.e., the number of months of cash left in bank if they continue at the current burn rate. The holidays of 2022 and new year of 2023 started with news from all over the world of companies in tech—big and small—cutting marketing spends and laying off employees. Edtech in India resorted to the same. In one way, it was a correction from the reckless, unsustainable spends they had signed up for during the pandemic, betting on large growth which never materialized.

Alongside this cost cutting, the companies were forced to look at their business models. When they were at a loss about how to make money, they resorted to chasing the demand which at that point was moving offline. So the companies started building offline learning centres. There is nothing wrong in moving with your customers; finally, the customers decide and if you are not where the customer is, then you are leaving them for your competitor. So, tweaking the strategy is fine, but the issue is the margin structure. Offline is a very different animal with high capex and much lesser margins when compared to online. The reasons why online ended up being attractive for the investors—easy to scale, low capex and high margins—were all forgotten with this shift in strategy. This pivot will make it all the more hard for these companies to reach the EBITDA commensurate with their current valuation and thus the only way out is to manage the business with whatever cash that comes your way. In other words, be cash positive, grow steadily and extend your runway. This in my view, is actually a good thing. I had realized, thanks to the many mentors I had, that while capital is essential for growth, excess capital can be very dangerous. An entrepreneur loses focus and gets carried away when there is too much capital. A good business is always built when the people running it treat money with respect, doing their utmost to get the best value out of it which then directly translates into giving the best service to your customer. Too much of capital makes you feel that you should not be spending time on small things like negotiating to get the best deal for your company and customers or using your vision and purpose rather than money to attract the best talent. You end up attracting a lot wrong people and overpaying them when you try to solve every problem by throwing money at it.

Chapter 24

The AI Teacher

On 1 May 2023, stock prices of Chegg, a US-based homework study website, fell by 40 per cent because of a statement made by its CEO during quarterly earnings that they have started seeing the impact of ChatGPT in their numbers (new account growth and sign-ups). With this, Chegg became one of the early casualties of the AI revolution. The impact on stock price was so dramatic because the market was expecting it for long.

Before looking at AI and ChatGPT, let's talk about Chegg. It was a company that made waves during Covid-19, when students en masse moved to remote learning. Chegg used its access to cheap but high-quality teachers in Asia particularly India to build one the most extensive homework help and step-wise textbook solutions. These were happily used by children the world over to do their homework. With lesser monitoring from teachers during Covid-19 years, kids were free to use Chegg extensively and soon it became widely accepted to use the website to complete one's homework and assignments. This helped the company grow their topline and bottomline extensively and their stock started trading at as high as $113 in February 2021 vs $29 in March 2020. As with all edtech during Covid-19 and post Covid-19, their business also fell when students returned to schools and universities. The stock traded at $24 in January 2022. But the worst was yet to come, and it did in the form of the ChatGPT onslaught which crashed its stock to $9.6 in May 2023.

ChatGPT (Chat Generative Pre-Trained Transformer) is an AI chatbot developed by Open AI, a company founded by ten engineers, along with Sam Altman (president of Y Combinator) and Elon Musk (founder of Tesla and Space X, among others) as board members, to take on the 'existential risk from AI'. The company used GPT models, especially GPT-3.5 and GPT-4, a type of large language model (LLM), to build the chatbot, which, with its detailed and articulate responses to every possible question asked to it quickly gained a high degree of acceptance. Though the answers were not always accurate and the fact that ChatGPT confidently responds misled some users, it was clearly the best option available in the market in this space. In some ways, it ended up competing with the most-used search engine, Google and YouTube (in case you want a video answer). Hence, education became one of the first-use cases the AI chat offered solutions to, impacting the company that was selling homework and textbook solutions, as the solutions were free and all the students had to do was open the ChatGPT4 chat window and copy-paste the question.

AI is a revolutionary idea for education; think about the millions of students who can now get their questions answered in a jiffy whenever they want and all they need is a good internet connection.

AI didn't stop there. There are several companies today that are working on LLM-based technologies which will generate precise solutions and even video solutions for a topic. Imagine, a student is able to create a teacher who looks the way they want, talks the way they want and instead of the AI chatbot churning out answers, they are done so by their favourite teacher, and that too all the while smiling to them from their mobile. It doesn't stop there, this AI teacher has the capability to pull out images, animations and even videos by experts pertaining to the questions the kid has asked. The 'unimaginable' possibilities of AI are imaginable and executable today. The question obviously is: will AI finally replace a human teacher?

To answer this question, let's break down the tasks done by our favourite teacher to drive outcomes at the student level:

- Take classes in an engaging manner with the help extensive knowledge and tools. This is largely content and articulation which AI can do.
- Understand student's strengths and weaknesses and motivate them to realize their true potential. This requires emotional intelligence and AI is still years away from doing this.
- Bring discipline and ensure students traverse through a structured learning schedule and close monitoring. AI can do the latter but can't act on the data to bring discipline.
- Bring together students as a community and facilitate peer learning and problem-solving. There is no way AI can do this.

Fundamentally, there is a lot more to learning than content. You will truly appreciate a teacher's irreplaceable contribution in a student's life if we look at learning holistically. At best, AI will be an enabler and help the best teachers handle a larger number of students thus solving the teacher scarcity problem we have today.

In an effort to use ChatGPT in a manner that enables learning, Khan Academy and BYJU's came up with learning chatbots which rather than giving solutions to the question, guides the students to find them. Let me explain with an example on how these bots respond to kids trying to get answers for their homework intelligently and make learning possible.

Student: Get me the answer for (7/12) × 2

(The student probably had to get the answer for the multiplication problem 7 divided by 12 multiplied by 2. In all possibility, they would have just copy-pasted the question on the bot chat from their homework sheet. Now let's look at how the chatbot responds.)

AI-powered chatbot: It's important that you learn how to do this yourself. What do you think you need to do to multiply 2 by 7/12?

Student: They need the same denominator.

AI-powered chatbot: That's a good thought and it's true when you are adding or subtracting such numbers. But in this case, you don't need to since you are multiplying. What else can you try?

As you can see, the bot is guiding the kid to the answer, step by step, encouraging them to think for themselves. Note that the AI, like a good and gentle teacher, corrected the student's understanding of the concept.

The possibilities this technology offers are remarkable, and I personally believe that combined with virtual reality, it will revolutionize the tools available to an educator and students to make learning a lot more accessible and of a far superior quality. Very soon, when a kid calls out his educator through Siri, an AI version of his favourite teacher will get projected on his Vision pro goggles. The AI teacher will then start a one-on-one doubt resolution session with the student based on that day's school lessons. And as always happens with technology, expensive Apple products will attract cheaper alternatives to the market creating deeper access with affordability. But all these are only possible if AI grows alongside the educator and does not try to replace the educator.

Chapter 25

The Future

In my attempt to write this book, I have spoken to educators who were cumulatively responsible for sending lakhs of students to IITs and other top universities and colleges. This includes people who were behind the largest coaching centres, early teachers of Kota, edtechs and influencers. To every teacher I met who claimed to me that they have created IITians, I asked the same question: 'Do you think it is possible to get a top JEE rank just through online coaching?' And every single time, I have got the same unequivocal answer: '100 per cent yes.' Each of them may have a different reason for the answer but seems like they were all clear that the future of education in India has online playing a crucial part in it. Let me recount a conversation with a teacher who started his coaching journey with V.K. Bansal and was part of the original Kota team.

'In the initial days of Kota, we were able to work with a repeater student and eventually he got rank one in JEE. It's all about the structure and process.' His words were music to my ears. Someone who has mentored lakhs of students from various parts of the country to help them reach their IIT goal is clear that the future is online. He continued, 'Finally a student learns through a series of moments of truth. A good teacher imparts this moment of knowledge through his style, tone, decibel and finds a way to resonate at the same frequency as the student's brain. That's when the knowledge in me travels to students. I can assure you that these things are replicable on a video and forget a human teacher, an AI teacher can learn these and become the perfect teacher personalized to the student who is listening to him.'

Everyone I spoke to believed that post Covid-19 going back to offline is a temporary lull in the unstoppable journey towards online. It was interesting to hear this conviction, but let's think through it. We no longer live in safe neighbourhoods where kids can freely move around in streets and villages, and parents needn't bother because the entire community knows each other and takes care of each other. Currently, we live in cities and towns where we try to confine our lives to our apartments and gated communities. Traffic is terrible and nobody likes to drop off their kids to a tuition class. Competition is only getting tougher and kids are taking supplementary coaching from Class V onwards. How do you, then, ensure you give that extra to your kids? Let them take it online! At least the disproportionate screen time they have now will be used for something useful.

Thanks to the realities of the world we are living in, online learning would incrementally become an option for students looking for tuitions and coaching. However, the pace was dramatically accelerated due to Covid-19. Today, parents across the country consider online learning as a mainstream alternative alongside neighbourhood offline centres. The reach that the online format was able to garner is remarkable. However, for a similar level of acceptability, more needs to be done. Let's look at some of the things we will need to concentrate on:

- Focus on outcomes. Parents and students come to us looking for a specific outcome. It could be doing better at school, cracking a competitive exam or getting a job.
- Outcomes come from delivery mechanisms which are engaging and interesting. Making this happen is the sole function of the edtech platform.
- The mode of delivery should depend on *what* you are teaching and *who* you are teaching. A 100-year-old concept can be best taught as a well-scripted video rich in animations by the best possible teacher. A constantly updating concept like ML algorithms will need an industry practitioner coming and doing a live session explaining the dynamics of how to apply it. A kid in school will need to be monitored closely online or offline ideally in partnership with parents, while a working professional can learn with limited mentoring.
- Every student learns at a different pace and has a unique natural learning inclination. Assessments, content and delivery styles should be personalized to make outcomes happen at every student level. This approach means that it's impossible to make money on every student. Disproportionate effort and a negative unit economics will be required to make weaker students excited about learning. Believe me, this is worth the spend because a life-changing intervention is always noticed and has the effect of a million-dollar marketing investment. I'm suggesting the opposite of Rankers and Bankers here!
- Take care of your customer—every one of them, and they will take care of your business!

The biggest advantage edtech companies have is the level of granularity and customization possible with the help of technology. It is extremely tough for an offline class to deliver outcomes to every student in the class. However, this is possible through customized learning journeys and differentiated interventions depending on the engagement level of the student. So far, we have just done one thing—created videos which can make classroom teaching interesting through visualization. In other words, we replicated classroom teaching as interesting videos. With this, we were able to excite a few kids who found the approach fresh compared to the 200-year-old teaching method using a blackboard and chalk. However, the excitement and engagement depleted soon, and the format lost its novelty. However beautiful a video you make, students will lose interest and move on to the next infatuation. That's how they are. They're young and have a restless mind. Sustainable engagement will need a lot more intervention than simple replication of classrooms in visual learning mode.

Research conducted by *Cognitive Science* in 1989 revealed that

- 10 per cent of people in the sample could learn by reading
- 20 per cent could learn by hearing (auditory learners)
- 30 per cent could learn by seeing (visual learners)
- 50 per cent could learn by hearing and seeing. This is what we do in classrooms and do more interestingly online

The striking insight from the survey was that 70 per cent of the people learn when they collaborate with their peers (communities) and 80 per cent learn when they actually do what they learn.

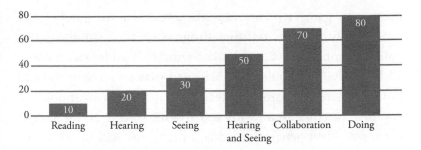

Different learning modes and their impact

Source: 'Self-explanations: How students study and use examples in
learning to solve problems'. *Cognitive Science*, 1989

Edtechs of tomorrow will need to solve for engagement by developing tools which will drive collaboration and learn by doing. Again, these things are hard to do in an offline environment. The best you can do in an offline B-school class is a case study group whose members will collaborate and learn. However, in practice, only those few interested in reading actually read the case and solve it by understanding the business situation the leader has been put in. In the online world, the best B-schools are converting the case studies into a simulation allowing the student to actually act as the CEO who goes through the situation—learn by doing and learn by making mistakes.

The same is true for K-12, test prep and higher education too. We are a country today with 360 million learners and 500 million gamers who spend several hours playing games like Ludo online. Imagine the impact on engagement that gamification can bring in. Games again cannot be used for each and every concept. There are some apps which do this and the product is just an overkill and waste of time. The best product will use games and simulation to teach the right concept. For example, think of a game which will make you solve for parallel and series combination of resistors. Progressive levels will throw out harder combinations and by the time the student completes all levels, he/she would have achieved mastery. The game will not end here as a single-player one; it will have options to compete or collaborate with your friend who is online on the platform. Next-generation edtech platforms will be all about putting in place the right medium to learn for every concept—asynchronous, live, games, simulation, assessment, assisted and even offline.

I really hope that time is not far when schools will start adopting these hybrid concepts in a big way. Imagine the efficacy we can bring in if we use the right tools and modes to teach basis the nature of topic. The practice if executed well in a collaborative environment can get the best out of the kids. I am not professing a pure online school here; I don't think is a good idea especially for smaller grades. There are a lot of things kids learn through collaboration and competition in the physical environment of school. However, hybrid and using online tools at the right places can be greatly beneficial. With hybrid, the whole concept of attendance can potentially get redefined from being physically present in the classroom to being mentally attentive in class.

The Confident Indian Youth

India currently is one of the fastest-growing economies in the world. Not only are we a powerhouse for services, we are slowly building our manufacturing prowess in certain niches. This emergence of new India is reflected in its youth too. Today's youth is high on self-confidence and no longer wants to follow the crowd when it comes to making decisions, whether it is purchase or education. This has resulted in diversification of career avenues from only engineering and medicine to broader options. Today, one can see us creating a large number of graduates in commerce, management, healthcare, arts, etc. This trend will gain more traction in the future and I won't be surprised if these domains become as large as engineering and medical soon. In one way, this is augmenting our ability to be the human-resource supplier of the world. Indian engineers (techies) and doctors are already in demand world over. Slowly the fields to which we supply high-skilled human resource is diversifying into management, finance and humanities. Some may call this brain drain, but I see it as advantage India since our education is providing opportunities to our people across the world even though we may not be able to do it in our country. Experience has shown that these people when really successful start giving back to the nation.

The self-confidence among Indians is no longer confined to big cities. Access to internet has ensured that aspirations and confidence percolate through to the nook and corner of the country. This has resulted in the need for skilling products in local languages. Along with support from the government, finally India has embarked on vocational-skills training in local languages. Today there are courses in full stack development, digital marketing, data science, stock trading, etc., which one can take up in a local language. This will open up hitherto backward communities where lack of English language skills was the biggest hinderance to a successful lifestyle transformation.

Upskilling 2.0

Thanks to NEP, higher education and upskilling have moved quickly in its journey online. With improving acceptance of higher education in hybrid and online mode, I expect a large part of master's and doctorate education moving online. This will allow our working professionals, a vast majority of whom starts working after graduation, to earn a postgraduate degree without taking a break from their well-paid jobs. When more practitioners come for postgraduate education, the universities and edtechs will be forced to make the curriculum more industry friendly and updated. This will start the irreversible movement towards platforms which will bring work and education together and truly start the revolution of lifelong learning.

I won't be surprised if government starts taking a more active role in this space considering the importance it holds in nation-building. One immediate impact of governments or government-backed institutions doing upskilling with quality, is that the price points will fall. The reduced price points, if used well, can open up the market in a big way thus making the essential product accessible to everyone deserving.

Building for the World

India boasts three key elements which are critical to building a large edtech ecosystem—high-calibre engineers, passionate and English-speaking teachers, and digitally skilled marketing, sales and operations talent. Not only does India possess these in abundance, we have it all available to us at a fraction of the cost they are available in the West. This makes Indian edtech ideal for building solutions for the entire world. This is already in action. Both Great Learning and UpGrad run worldwide online partnerships of multiple US and European universities. Sitting here, these companies admit students to online programmes of these universities from across the world.

For a nation of a billion-plus, implementing efficacy and efficiency in education through technology cannot be a novelty, it is a necessity. There is no way we can find millions of motivated and talented teachers who can train the 360 million learners waiting to spread their wings. Hence, we have to use every aspect of technology to make learning engaging and entertaining. I believe the current reversal is temporary and there are no demand-side problems. Today, parents and students are looking at online lectures as a mainstream option alongside offline ones. The problems we see today are all internal issues of the edtech companies.

We are also at a crossroads in this journey. We have time and again shown our capability to build a great edtech story, but our tearing hurry to make it happen has left the sector plagued with reverses. With failures we all learn, and so have our edtech entrepreneurs. Today, I find them more mature and ready to take things structured and steady, not slow but at the right pace to build learning and deliver outcomes. This new-found maturity will form the foundation for future edtech enterprises which will educate the billion!

Acknowledgements

This book grew out of years of experience in education and is a testimony to their several students who I was lucky to teach. I owe to them my understanding of education process.

There are several people who played very important roles in my career, mentoring me at various stages in my life. Heartfelt thanks to Byju Raveendran and Ronnie Screwvala for trusting me with such large responsibilities at an early age. The founding group of BYJU'S and the co-founders of upGrad Mayank Kumar and Phalgun K. were a few other people who were my partners throughout the edtech journey. Without their support and comradeship, there would have been little success.

I would also like to thank Penguin for helping me put this book together, especially Radhika Marwah and Manali Das.

Above all, thanks to my wife, Surbhi, who has been a companion in the ups and downs of life and has been the bouncing board for ideas, always. If not for her managing the kids and family along with her own start-up, The Mom Store, and giving me time to pursue my career, this book wouldn't have been a reality.